Letters from the Fens

Letters from
the Fens

EDWARD STOREY

Illustrated by Helen Hale

ROBERT HALE · LONDON

Robert Hale Limited
Clerkenwell House
Clerkenwell Green
London EC1R 0HT

2 4 6 8 10 9 7 5 3 1

Typeset by
Derek Doyle & Associates, Mold, Flintshire.
Printed in Great Britain by
St Edmundsbury Press Limited, Bury St Edmunds
and bound by
WBC Book Manufacturers Limited, Bridgend

ꙮ Contents ꙮ

✶ Acknowledgements ✶

Once again I am deeply grateful to the many people in the Fens who have helped me with their own knowledge, interests, letters and documents, which were essential to the completion of this book. They certainly made the research for each of the subjects an enjoyable pursuit, even though the actual writing of the Letters was sometimes a problem.

My thanks especially to Miss Dian Blawer, Dr Peter Cave and his wife Margaret, Mr Peter Clayton, the Misses D. and P. Dix, Mr George Dixon, Mr Ken Duller, Mr Barry Ferguson, Mrs Bridget Holmes, Mr Norman Leveritt and the Spalding Gentlemen's Society, Mrs Betty Spridgeon, Miss Christina Swaine and the Staff at Peckover House, and to Mr Arthur Wing.

I am also indebted to the Matron, Mr Newton Wills and the staff at the Sue Ryder Home, Thorpe Hall, Peterborough, to the Curator and staff at the Wisbech and Fenland Museum and, not least, to the Peterborough Central Library's Local Studies Room.

I wish, too, to express my appreciation of Helen Hale's readiness to respond to my requests for particular illustrations, all of which add their own quality to the text.

Finally, I have to say that my wife and friends had to put up with my constant fear of missing the last post, especially towards the end of writing these Letters, so I thank them for their support, tolerance and encouragement. I can do no more than dedicate this book to all who were part of its making.

✍ Introduction ✍

When I decided on the title of this book, even before I began writing it, I had no idea that it would be misunderstood or cause confusion. When I told my friends that it was to be called *Letters from the Fens*, I was surprised to be asked 'Whose letters?' and 'Where are you getting them from?' One even went so far as to say 'So *you* are not actually writing the book, only editing it!' Those who thought I had discovered original letters written by Edith Cavell, Thomas Clarkson, Octavia Hill, Sir Harry Smith, or any of the other personalities included in these pages, were clearly disappointed when I explained that *I* was writing the letters, saying 'Oh, you mean, you are making them up and pretending to be those people!'

So some explanation was needed, and probably still is, as you start to read this volume. The Letters are, in a way, made up, because that is what writing is all about. They are my letters and I wrote them, but they are about real people who lived in the Fens and are based on fact. They are, if you like, mini-biographies of men and women I have grown to admire over the years and now wish to see better known beyond our parish boundaries.

But why Letters? Why not chapters? The simple answer to that is that I wanted my chapters to be more personal – to be written more to individuals, like letters, rather than detached essays directed to an anonymous readership. What I knew I had to avoid was letting this relaxed, intimate style of presentation drift into chattiness or trivia. I wanted the Letters to be taken seriously and be seen as part of the whole chronicle of Fenland life.

The idea came to me because, over the twenty-seven years that I have been writing about the Fens, scores of readers have written to me asking questions such as 'What, or who, was the Whittlesey Straw Bear?' or 'Is it true that Thomas Clarkson was the main instigator in the movement for the abolition of the Slave Trade?' and

'What else did Octavia Hill do besides start the National Trust?'

Some of these letters came from New Zealand, Spain, Italy, Australia and Canada, from people whose parents or grandparents had gone to live in those countries half a century or more ago. Some wrote to me because they were working on a project for school or, like the young lady from Milan University, writing a thesis on the relationship between a particular landscape and its people – in her case, the Fens. For practical reasons I could not always give the complete answer I would have liked to give, so a book seemed to be the best way of finding the space required for those details excluded from my more immediate replies.

It is not an original idea. Other travel books have been presented in the form of correspondence, as indeed have some novels. The Scottish writer John Macky published his *A Journey Through England: In Familiar Letters* in this fashion in three volumes from 1714 to 1723. To some extent Daniel Defoe did the same in his *A Tour Thro' the Whole Island of Great Britain* from 1724 to 1727 and I always feel that William Cobbett's *Rural Rides* read as personal letters, rather than just social history or good topography. It is rather like sending a friend instalments of a journal that one has kept for a particular journey or year. There are personal touches as well as facts.

These Letters of mine were written in the twelve months from January to December 1997. Although I would not claim them to be in strict chronological order, or even a complete record of the events of that year, they do follow the seasons and local customs as they unfold in the lives of Fenland people. So, the first Letter is about the Whittlesey Straw Bear Day, which happens only once a year in January; similarly the Letter about John Peck could only be set in August, and the story of the World Conker Championship placed in no other month than October. In this way the book does have a pattern to it and becomes its own diary. On the other hand, the Letter about the family of Russian refugees, the Pestereffs, took several months to put together and belongs to the whole rather than the part.

In the writing of these Letters I have discovered many things about the Fens of which I knew very little, or nothing. So I am grateful that the questions were asked in the first place, and that eventually I was able to answer them. It proves, yet again, that we can never know all there is to know about something we have previously taken for granted. Some of the Letters are not necessarily about a place or a person but are simply reflections on my own relationship with a landscape that has so far been my whole life and the source of all my writing. These, too, are all part of the year's journey and discovery.

However successful or unsuccessful they may prove to be, I think I also wanted to do something to restore the lost art of letter-writing. It is so easy now to pick up the telephone, or to fax a message, that we no longer sit down to rediscover the actual pleasure of writing a long letter by hand to someone. I still find enormous satisfaction in writing with a fountain-pen and like to believe something of me goes into the letters my friends receive.

It is true that these days much of what we communicate can be preserved in other ways, but it was not always so, and we should be grateful that John Keats, Jane Carlyle, Dorothy Wordsworth, Jane Austen, Sir Walter Scott, Charles Dickens and many other writers of the eighteenth and nineteenth centuries, did not have access to such technological marvels as we have at our disposal today. Our literature would be much impoverished without their correspondence, which is nearly always as well-written and as entertaining as their works which were intended for publication. Many of these writers wrote thousands of letters a year and, when collected – as most of them are now – several volumes are needed to accommodate them.

Good letters should read like conversations on the page. But this does not mean that they have to be trite or gossipy; they can be informative as well as entertaining, discreet and sometimes even indiscreet. Some writers may write letters to friends in the hope that the world is looking over their shoulders, but one cannot always be sure that such letters will necessarily be kept by their recipients. I wonder how much intimate knowledge or wisdom has been inadvertently (or, for that matter, deliberately) consigned to the flames, either through embarrassment or neglect?

These Letters, by the very nature of their existence in book form, were written with the unashamed intention of having them published, but I trust that I have managed to retain something of the spirit of the letter by making them personal and honest, and that their contents will have some interest to all who read them. More than one reader will, I think, recognize that a particular letter is addressed to them, because of the questions they asked me, but I would also like to believe that there are quite a few other readers who will feel that the replies apply equally to anyone interested in the history of the Fens.

By accepting this challenge I hope I have produced a further record of the life and achievements of Fenland people during the last two or three hundred years. Without the efforts of these earlier dwellers we should not have the Fens we have today. They are all part of our history and, as these later pages will reveal, may well be seen as the last true survivors of a vanishing world that will conclude the dramatic story of the Fens. There is not only a change in the climate but a change in the inhabitants of this once remote and singularly independent kingdom where men and women fought for their existence and individual dignity. Whatever happens in the future, the Fens will never be the same as the Fen-country we shall have lost. Man, as well as nature, will see to that.

E.S.
December 1997

✑ 1 ✑

A Straw Bear and the Stars

If, for some incomprehensible reason, you found yourself in the Fenland town of Whittlesey on a bleak, misty morning at the beginning of January, you would probably be puzzled to see the streets already lined three-deep with people puffing clouds of breath into the frosty air as if they were all pretending to be steam trains waiting to be off. And, if your curiosity got the better of you, and you managed to get one of those impatient spectators to explain, you would soon find out why they were waiting there in their anoraks, wax-jackets, good old-fashioned overcoats, woolly hats and scarves.

In fairness, I think I should tell you that you would only witness such a scene on this one Saturday morning of the year, and in this one town. And, even if the explanation was a bit slow or incoherent in coming, you would not have to wait long before you found out why these good-humoured and foot-jigging folk were anxiously looking at their watches. For, at some time between ten-thirty and ten-forty, you would hear the distant beating of drums, or the piercing curlew-cry of a penny whistle. You might even hear a ripple of tinkling bells and the shuffle of clogs. At the same time a growing buzz of excitement would run like an electric charge through each row of people, who were suddenly not as cold as they had felt five minutes ago. For this would be the beginning of the parade that is part of the famous Whittlesey Straw Bear Festival, when people from miles around come to join in this annual and ancient ceremony which was revived in 1980.

The procession alone now attracts well over two hundred participants, who appear in a bizarre array of costumes based on folklore traditions. As well as the magnificent, tall Straw Bear itself – of

13

The Whittlesey straw bear and musician

which I will tell you more in a moment – there are a few other larger-than-life-size creatures. This year we had what I think was a cockerel and a two-legged reindeer. As well as the motley collection of dancers there were the musicians – accordion-players, penny-whistle-blowers, drummers and the odd trombone. I don't suppose the trombonist would approve of my using the word *odd*, but you know what I mean. I am not sure whether such an instrument would have featured in the festival five hundred years ago, but we are not perfectionists in these matters, and I suppose sackbuts and krummhorns are harder to come by these days. There were also, as usual, some rather well-fed 'peasants' and cherubic 'urchins' in push-chairs. In fact, the Straw Bear Day is now a delightful mixture of a carnival parade and a circus, as well as the re-enactment of a genuine piece of folklore. It's all jolly good fun and is keeping alive something of medieval England, the Morris Men, the Molly Dancers and the occasional hobby-horse all adding to the spectacle.

So you would soon appreciate why the people had been waiting expectantly for the procession to arrive and make its way from the Ivy Leaf Club to the Market Place with its seventeenth-century Buttercross. Eventually the procession, led by the Straw Bear, moves off on its round of at least a dozen local pubs and a few nursing homes. Many of the spectators will follow, either to keep warm or to take advantage of the pubs being open all day.

The names of some of the groups taking part also have a ring of 'Olde England' about them – King's Men Morris, Red Leicester, White Rose, Pig Dyke, Cross Keys Clog, Stevenage Sword and Seven Champions. Teams from many parts of the country come to share in the celebrations of this unique occasion, from Huddersfield, Norwich, Nottingham, King's Lynn, Stevenage and Peterborough.

Having watched these activities, it seems to me that you need several qualifications to take part. You need the ability to throw off any inhibitions you may have; the ability to dress up in some weird and wonderful costume; the ability to go on dancing, playing, hop-skip-and-jumping for hours; and, last but not least, the ability to quaff a few tankards of good ale as you frolic from pub to pub.

Now who, in this darkest time of the year, when the weather is so inhospitable, so limb-chilling and soul-crippling, could ever blame anyone for wanting to warm both body and spirit so generously? After all, one of the reasons for this New Year festival is to celebrate the rejuvenation of life.

I have a feeling you're saying that it's about time I explained what the Straw Bear is really all about and why it was revived by the Whittlesea Society in 1980, after a lapse of some seventy years. (By the way, don't be confused by the two different spellings of the town name. The suffixes *ea* or *ey* both mean the same, and signify that Whittlesey was once an island. The railway station, the local history society and a few people like myself, still prefer to see it spelt with *ea*.)

I am sometimes asked if the revival of this winter festival has managed to retain the spirit of the original custom. I can't answer that, because we have no reliable records of what the earliest festivals would have been like. The beginnings of the Straw Bear go back to pagan or druid times, and much of what we associate with it today – such as the morris dancing – is, by comparison, fairly recent, having been introduced into this country probably during the reign of Edward III as a variation of the Moorish dancing which was then popular on the continent.

I am pretty certain that today's Straw Bear Day is a much more sophisticated affair than it was at the turn of the century when it was threatened with extinction. That it did not quite go through with its death throes is confirmed by the following extract I received from a friend just a few days ago, which he had found in The Folklore Society's journal of 1910. A gentleman in Sheffield recalled:

> When I was at Whittlesey (Cambridgeshire) yesterday, [12 Jan 1909], I had the pleasure of meeting a 'straw bear', if not two, in the street. I had not been in Whittlesey on the day for nearly forty years and feared the custom had died out. In my boyhood the 'straw bear' was a man completely swathed in straw, led by a string by another and made to dance in front of people's houses, in return for which money was expected. This always took place on the Tuesday following Plough-Monday. Yesterday the 'straw bear' was a boy and I saw no dancing . . .

In those days it was much more of a purely local event than it is today, and sometimes things did get a bit out of hand, much to the irritation of the townspeople and the police – a fact remembered by the correspondent from Sheffield:

> I was told that two years ago a zealous inspector of police had forbidden 'straw bears' as a form of cadging, and my informant said

that he thought that in many places they had been stopped by the police . . .

Whittlesey was one of the very few places in Britain to keep the custom alive as long as it did. Even now, with its revival, I believe it is the sole survivor. (I think I am also right in saying that in Cambridgeshire only Ramsey once had a similar event, and their Straw Bear Day was held on Plough Monday rather than the traditional Tuesday following it.) Until recent times Whittlesey always celebrated its own day on the Tuesday after Plough Monday (which was the first Monday after Twelfth Night). With its revival it seemed to make sense to move it to the first Saturday after Twelfth Night, so that many more people could attend the weekend's activities. So who said we were resistant to change?

Change is something few of us can avoid. Times have certainly changed for farm-workers since Plough Monday was once a regular, and sometimes feared, ritual at the beginning of the year. When you start delving through the history books there are several references to Plough Monday, going back to the thirteenth century, but its roots, like those of the Straw Bear, are doubtless buried in unrecorded time.

Whatever its origins, it was nearly always an excuse for carefree merry-making, taking liberties, and probably getting drunk to offset the miseries of winter and unemployment. It also gave some of the local farm lads an opportunity to get their own back on farmers or landlords against whom they had a particular grudge. As they went round the town with their decorated hand-drawn ploughs and blackened faces, mainly to entertain and collect money for their feast at the end of the day, they also intimidated some of the townspeople with threats of ploughing up their front gardens or doorsteps unless a generous contribution was made to the funds. It was not uncommon for some vandals to carry out threats of violence without necessarily having a bone to pick with any particular person. Magistrates and masters were high on the list; it is quite amazing how courageous one can be behind a mask or in a fancy costume. I remember years ago hearing a story about a local doctor who decided to disguise himself as one of the black-faced ploughboys to find out exactly who the ringleaders were. But the men soon found out who he was and tied him up against the cemetery gates until their deeds were done.

But that is all a long time ago now, and I can assure you that today's Straw Bear Festival is good clean fun, an orderly if not refined affair. The merry-making is conducted in the right spirit, and a timeless tradition is now being preserved for the right reasons. The festival actually starts on the Friday evening with a folk concert, given this year by the Old Rope String Band, and it ends on the Sunday afternoon with the final ceremony of burning the Bear.

Now you may wonder why such an elaborate costume, which takes months to make, should not be kept for the following year. The answer is simple. You cannot carry its luck, good or bad, from one year to another – and, if the best must always be sacrificed to the gods, even a pagan god, then the best straw of each year's harvest should be kept to go into its making. So when the Straw Bear has done its duty the straw is offered to the flames, and next summer must dress its own bear in its own straw.

Yes, yes, I can hear you saying, but you still haven't given us a reason for all this ritual, for all these strange and boozy goings-on. What is it for, and who started it in the first place?

Well, I have to confess that I have been prevaricating, putting off the moment of truth because, quite frankly, no one is really at all sure what the truth is. You see, the origins of the Straw Bear are lost in those shadowy corners of antiquity, and the reasons for its first appearances are obscure, as with most of our traditional celebrations.

We have known for a long time that such rituals were essential to country people's respect for the land, in the same way that superstition and magic were, especially in pre-Christian times when every folk-dance was a kind of incantation, every straw dolly a charm. To a lesser degree, perhaps, we still believe in them, and the 'earth spirit' conditions our behaviour more than we think.

Although Straw Bears were to become rare in England, they had been known in other parts of Europe for many centuries, in Germany, Russia and Scandinavia. So the Whittlesey Straw Bear has very real links with a past that is now mostly forgotten, and if for some incomprehensible reason you were to find yourself in this town on a cold January day when these old customs are being re-enacted, I hope you will stay to join the waiting crowds and enjoy the light-hearted revelries. It is worth it, if only to applaud the brave person dressed up inside the massive straw image that looks so convincing, so real, that he might have just stepped out of the dark pages of a folk-tale that has been told for more than two thousand years. That costume, incidentally, adds about five stone to the wearer's weight – I would imagine that he sleeps well that night.

I for one was ready to get back to the warmth of home before it grew dark. The only time that I really enjoy winter darkness now is when the frosty sky is gleaming with those thousands of sparkling stars that were visible even before the first Straw Bear was thought of, when ancient man looked up to the heavens for his mysteries and his hope.

Stars always intrigued me as a child. Often, when I had been put safely to bed and the light was turned out, I would wrap myself in the eiderdown and go to sit by the little window of my room, to stare up in wonder at the vast sky, waiting to see if any of the stars would move or fall to earth. When one did occasionally slip swiftly out of place I would pull the eiderdown up over my ears, certain that at any moment the star would come sizzling down through the dark, to explode in our back garden. Instead it fizzled out silently into space, and I was left wondering if it was true that whenever I saw a falling star someone in the neighbourhood died.

But how much longer shall we be able to see the stars, I ask? I was reading in one of the national newspapers just before Christmas that astronomers are already protesting (and rightly so) that the Millennium Commission's plans to illuminate hundreds of public buildings in the year 2000 will intensify light pollution to such an extent that the night sky will cease to exist for people on earth. And, what is worse, the effect will probably deprive children in the future of ever seeing stars at all. Even now, in our towns and cities, it is virtually impossible to see a truly star-lit night, and when we do go out into the country to find a relatively unspoilt sky, it is something of a revelation to see so many stars still glistening in their eternal places. Now, I don't suppose I should have used that word 'eternal' because, like you, I am well aware that we are only just receiving the light of some of those stars which burnt themselves out thousands of years ago, but they *feel* everlasting.

I was talking to a lady yesterday who made me feel quite envious. She said her nearest street lamp was four miles away, so she was still able to enjoy the same winter skies she had known as a child. Not many can. When did you last see the full breadth and majesty of the Milky Way, or express wonder at seeing the whole of the Pleiades? Certainly not as clearly as we did even forty years ago. So why make it worse? And just imagine how lost the Magi would be if, in another two thousand years' time, they were told to follow a star which they could no longer see. Well, I agree, such a fanciful argument doesn't hold water these days. Yet, how easy it is to take things for granted, to let things slip from our grasp and disappear into artificiality or the non-existent. I want neither the Straw Bear nor the Great Bear to disappear.

So, at the beginning of this old New Year, I urge you to enjoy whatever is out there, in sky or furrow, by meadow or stream, for we are possibly counting the days. And, who knows, on such a moonlit night you might also glimpse the transparent, wraith-like form of the very first Straw Bear. Only then, maybe, are you likely to know how it all began.

〜 2 〜

A Hero and a Spanish Lady

Anyone driving from Whittlesey to March, along Eastrea Road, could be forgiven for raising a bemused eyebrow at seeing a Community College named after a certain Harry Smith. Now I hasten to say that I have known several decent, law-abiding and honourable Harry Smiths in my time, but it is not a name that immediately springs to mind when wanting to give a distinguished title to an important building, library or school – unless, of course, that famous person has also distinguished himself in some particular and memorable way.

If manners maketh the man, perhaps the deed maketh the name. At least that is how it was with the Harry Smith that I am going to tell you about, and why you will soon understand how the Community College in Whittlesey came to be named after him. In passing, I will also tell you that the building and its grounds stand where the old Whittlesea Workhouse once stood. I can remember that sad place being pulled down, and when I went to school we were taken down to work in the neglected gardens where once the paupers had worked; we were, I think, growing radishes and parsnips to help the war effort. I regret to say that those afternoons of labour did not turn me into a gardener.

However, let me get back to Sir Harry and give you his full title – Sir Harry George Wakelyn Smith, Bt, GCB, Hero of Aliwal and Governor of the Cape of Good Hope. He was born in Whittlesey on 28 June 1787 (and not 1788, as is sometimes given). Sir Harry himself was never certain of his age and added or subtracted two or three years throughout his life. He left the year of his birth blank in the manuscript of his autobiography, but the baptismal register states that he was born in 1787.

However, no date can alter the fact that he was born in St Mary's

Street, Whittlesey, and the house is now called Aliwal House. He also has a pub named after him, as well as a Community College, and the events of his life more than match those of Lawrence of Arabia. The opening sentences of his autobiography begin at the beginning and set the matter-of-fact tone for what follows:

> I was born in the parish of Whittlesey and County of Cambridgeshire in the year [1787]. I am one of eleven children, six sons and five daughters. Every pain was taken with my education which my father could afford, and I was taught natural philosophy, classics, algebra, and music.

His mother in fact had fourteen children, but three died before reaching maturity; Sir Harry was thinking only of those who survived – an error he was to make sometimes in his military career. His father, John Smith, was a local surgeon, and his mother was the daughter of the local vicar.

At the age of seventeen he joined the Whittlesea Troop of Yeoman Cavalry and one of his first assignments was to patrol at the Norman Cross prisoner-of-war camp, where French and allied prisoners were held in captivity during the Napoleonic Wars from 1793 to 1815. It was a modest beginning and Sir Harry recalls that his slight physique as a young man provoked one of the prisoners into teasing him – 'I say, leetel fellow, go home with your Mama; you must eat more pudding.'

Slight of build he may have been, but he soon proved that he was strong, adventurous and a superb horseman who could tame even the wildest charger he was given. He was soon recruited into the newly-created Corps of riflemen, known as the Green Jackets, and almost overnight acquired the rank of second lieutenant.

Leaving the comforts of home for a lifetime in the army, where most of his service was to be overseas, was not easy, and he began to have doubts about the career he had chosen. He tells us that at his last dinner at home he:

> bore up manfully, then ran to the stables to say goodbye to Jack, a beautiful little horse I had reared from a foal and who, in the hunting field, had kept me ahead of all the others. I threw my arms round his neck and had a good cry.

It would have been impossible for anyone then to imagine such a sensitive young man becoming a fearless, and at times ruthless, soldier who survived some 400 skirmishes in the wars of the Americas, Africa, India and Spain and fought some particularly bloody battles for the Duke of Wellington.

Sir Harry's anxious mother also made it difficult to break with home, and he relates how she 'wept awfully' when the moment of departure came. He also says that she asked two favours of him: first, that he should never visit a public billiard room, and second, that whenever he met the enemy he should always remember that he was born a true Englishman.

Between that leave-taking in 1805 and returning to his native town to be buried in 1860 is a story that would be difficult to believe in, even in fiction. No *Boy's Own* epic could produce such a sequence of hair-raising and heroic deeds, defying all odds, all natural laws, and death itself.

I will not burden you now with a complete chronicle of his exploits, his victories, failures, defeats and triumphs. His two-volume autobiography – published posthumously in 1901 by John Murray – would, if you could find a copy, keep you entertained for hours. Joseph Lehmann's biography *Remember You Are An Englishman* – published by Jonathan Cape in 1977 – is more easily obtainable and gives an excellent portrait of this unpredictable, complex, stubborn and charismatic soldier from Whittlesey. The danger with heroes is that we can forget that they were also human and had their weaknesses as well as their strengths.

All I can do in this letter to you today is highlight some of Sir Harry's campaigns and keep you in suspense a little longer over the most romantic part of his extraordinary life. Although his own account is very lengthy, incomplete and not always accurate (because his handwriting was not easy to read), it has a freshness and an intimacy that I found riveting. I think I ought to say that I am not the slightest bit interested in war or war stories, but these two volumes do belong to that category of books called 'un-put-downables'. Professor Lehmann's biography is much more professional and succinct, but you get the feeling that the story is (under-standably) coming to you second-hand – as, indeed, is this appetizer of mine. If you can by any chance read both accounts simultane-ously, as I have done, you will get the best of both worlds.

So, briefly, this is how the events of his life unfolded, with a speed that outstripped that of his favourite charger. In June 1806 he embarked for service under Sir Samuel Auchmuty in South America, helping to capture Montevideo. In July of that year he took part in the attack on Buenos Aires, which ended disastrously for the British, and he returned to England in December 1807.

The following year he embarked for the Peninsular War and landed at Corunna to help Sir John Moore. In May 1809 he set sail for Lisbon to serve under Lieutenant-Colonel Beckwith and Brigadier-General Craufurd, but he was seriously wounded in action near Almeida and was forced to convalesce.

In 1811 he was appointed Brigade-Major and saw action at Sabugal, Fuentes de Onoro and the storming of Ciudad Rodrigo. He also took part in the ignominious and costly sacking of Badajoz. That city was pounded for days by Wellington's guns whilst 15,000 men waited to attack the seven main strongholds of the city walls. The order to attack came on the night of 6 April, and even the young buglers were begging to be in this 'great and glorious battle'. It was neither; the following morning 1,500 troopers lay dead, or so seriously wounded that they were left to die. Many more were burned or trampled to death, and Sir Harry found nine of his best young officers among those who had been sacrificed. For two more days the remnant of that once optimistic army battered away at the city until it surrendered.

It was then that the British, and Portuguese, troops behaved so disgracefully against the defenceless citizens of Badajoz – people they had come to liberate. Thankful to have survived the battle, and quick to celebrate their victory, the men went on the rampage, getting more drunk and violent by the minute. Their commanding officers were helpless to control their lusts. Women caught in the tumult were raped and mutilated; priests, nuns and children were crazily murdered and houses looted. Sickened by what he had seen, Sir Harry wrote:

> The atrocities committed by our soldiers on the poor innocent and defenceless inhabitants of the city, no words suffice to depict. Civilized man, when let loose and the bonds of morality relaxed, is a far greater beast than the savage, more refined in his cruelty, more fiend-like in every act; and oh, too truly did our heretofore noble soldiers disgrace themselves.

And yet, added Sir Harry in his typically selfish way:

> this scene of debauchery, however cruel to many, to me has been the solace and the whole happiness of my life for thirty-three years.

How, you may well ask, could a famous and sensitive Englishman find solace in such a memory of bestiality? To answer that question I must now tell you about the romantic episode in his story and how he married his Spanish lady – Juana María de los Dolores de León, who at the time was no more than a girl, a 'poor defenceless maiden of thirteen, who was thrown upon my generous nature through her sister', as Sir Harry puts it in his *Memoirs*.

Despite the behaviour of the British soldiers, several of the women who survived – especially those of some aristocratic background – fled to the British commanding officers and pleaded for protection. Among them were two sisters. Sir Harry's fellow officer, Sir John Kincaid, recounted the scene vividly in his own autobiography *Random Shots from a Rifleman* (1835), and Sir Harry could do no better than quote from it:

> I was conversing with a friend the day after at the door of his [Harry's] tent, when we observed two ladies coming towards us; they seemed both young, and when they came near, the elder of the two threw back her mantilla to address us . . . . She at once addressed us in that confident, heroic manner so characteristic of the high-bred Spanish maiden, told us who they were – the last of an ancient and honourable house – and then referred to an officer high in rank in our army for the truth of her tale. . . . Her house, she said, was a wreck; and, to show the indignities to which they had been subjected, she pointed to where the blood was still trickling down their necks, caused by the wrenching of their ear-rings through the flesh by the hands of worse than savages. For herself, she said, she cared not; but for the agitated and almost unconscious maiden by her side she was in despair.

Sir John elaborates the story more than I have time to do here, but it is quite clear that he had immediately fallen in love with this young girl. She was to him 'more transcendingly lovely' than any woman he had ever seen. 'To look at her was to love her.'

The trouble was that Sir Harry had also fallen in love with her and thought her 'Nature's fairest and most delicate moulding, the figure of an angel, with an eye of light and an expression which then inspired me with a maddening love.'

Juana had, in fact, just turned fourteen, and Harry found in her 'an understanding superior to her years'. He was then twenty-four and decided not to risk losing her to anyone else. Although she was a devout Catholic, straight from a convent, and he was a staunch Fenland Protestant, he asked Wellington for permission to marry her. The Duke not only agreed but consented to give the bride away at the hastily arranged marriage service conducted by an Irish Catholic chaplain. Far from it being a disaster waiting to happen it was to be what Sir Harry claimed it to be – 'the whole happiness of my life'. Juana was to remain his constant companion throughout his many campaigns until his death. She survived him by twelve years.

The marriage was only the beginning of their long and enthralling story but I fear it is all I have time to tell you in this letter. If you would like to know more of what happened next I could continue the narrative at some later date. Just let me know.

There is, however, one question I shall not be able to answer, and that is, what became of Juana's sister? From all the accounts I have read it would seem that, having made sure Juana was safe, she just disappeared. Wasn't there, I wonder, any other British officer willing to do the same for her?

Like all good stories, I suppose there is only room for one heroine. The events that coloured the lives of the Smiths are as much as the imagination can cope with, even these days. What annoys me is that I didn't hear about all these things when I was at school. Maybe we had different heroes then.

ও 3 ও

Return of the Soldier

It came as no surprise to me the other day when I heard that you wished me to continue with the story of Sir Harry Smith and his young bride Juana – and, of course, I am happy to do so. What I was going to write to you about can wait. If your imagination has been aroused why delay our return to Spain?

Needless to say, there was no honeymoon for the young newly-weds. Sir Harry boasted that he never took the leave he was entitled to and did not know what holidays were. He was a full-time soldier engaged in war, and duty came first. Fortunately for him, his wife agreed with that attitude, as he explains in his autobiography:

> My duty was my duty – I gloried in it; my wife even still more so, and never did she say 'you might have been with me', or complain if I was away. On the contrary, after many a day's fatiguing march, when I sought her out, her first question invariably was, 'Are you sure you have done all your duties?' *Then* I admit my attention was unbounded and we were happy.

Despite the fact that he was often riding up to sixty miles a day and, when he was not fighting battles, loved to go hunting, Sir Harry still had enough strength for an energetic sex life and made love to Juana not only in his tent but often under the stars at night when they slept in the open.

It must have been a dramatic change of life for this quiet, angelic girl from a convent to be suddenly plunged into a world of men, horses, guns, bugles, battles, hare-coursing and constant swearing (Sir Harry was known to use every word in the soldier's vocabulary, and his massive, megaphonic voice could be heard booming across any battlefield when he needed to shout.) Not only did she have to adjust to this very masculine world, she also had to learn how to ride, which was something she had not done as a girl. Being of strong character, she wanted no concessions. She wanted her husband's own thoroughbred Arab stallion. Understandably, he wouldn't let her have it. They argued. (Indeed they argued a great deal throughout their married life, because they both had the 'quickest of tempers'. But, equally, they were, wrote Sir Harry, 'both ready to forgive and both intoxicated with happiness'.) She got the Arab.

One of the first battles Juana witnessed from her husband's side was at Salamanca on 22 July 1812. It was to be Wellington's most outstanding victory against the odds. In forty minutes an army of 40,000 was defeated and the approach to Madrid established. And, in Madrid, they were to wash, buy clothes, have dinner-parties and attend candle-lit balls. The now dazzling, vivacious and elegantly dressed Juana became the darling of the Division and Sir Harry was a very proud, unjealous husband.

But soon all this excitement and reprieve from war was to end. In May 1814 Sir Harry was appointed Adjutant-General to the force which had been sent under Major-General Ross to continue the war in America. There he took part in the capture and burning of Washington and the fiercer battle for New Orleans. In 1815 he returned to England to rejoin his wife but had to proceed immediately to the Netherlands. It seems that England was at war with someone in almost every other part of the world.

Sir Harry was, however, pleased to be serving again under Wellington and distinguished himself at Waterloo. He was then chosen to lead the march on Paris, thrilled by the display of British colours following him. In the June of that year he was awarded the Waterloo Medal and breveted as Lieutenant-Colonel. He was still only twenty-eight.

One would have thought he deserved a few weeks' leave after that campaign, but the ambitious young Harry did not want to be missing if any other honours were to be won. When he returned to England in 1818 he was posted to serve with the 2nd battalion of the Rifle Brigade on duty in Ireland.

There was to be little rest for Sir Harry for at least another thirty years. After a brief lull he was sent, first to Jamaica in 1826, then, two years later, to the Cape of Good Hope. In 1835 he was put in charge of the colony and at once rode from Cape Town to Grahamstown, a distance of 700 miles over rough country, in the incredibly short time of six days. (I feel that my own narrative is moving at almost the same pace, but you will appreciate, I hope, that I am only giving you the bare bones of a story that takes volumes. It still puzzles me that the story is not better known, even locally. Maybe if a big-screen movie could be made and become a box-office attraction, things would be different.)

Throughout the next few months Sir Harry was to fight many battles with the Kaffirs, personally taking on their great warrior-chief Hintza, who was eventually killed trying to hide in a river. These were the years that Harry established his reputation for bravery and leadership. He rode with his men and was always the first to draw his sword.

But I must leap ahead yet again to the year 1846 and the battle that was to become synonymous with the name of Sir Harry Smith and earn him his claim to immortality – Aliwal, in India. He had received orders from Lord Hill early in 1840 to proceed to that troubled country and assume the post of Adjutant-General to Her Majesty's forces, where he also had the local rank of Major-General. Within a week Harry and Juana were on board the *David Scott*, sailing from the Cape of Good Hope to begin what is perhaps the most memorable chapter in a military career.

The one thing that can always be said about Sir Harry is that he never lacked confidence. He was not a modest man – some even thought him a braggart. In one of his letters to his sister Alice he had written 'My heart sickens with ambition', and he fervently believed that if a problem could be solved, or a battle won, he was the only man for the job. But the first years in India frustrated him because he was not being given many jobs, responsibilities or commands to keep him busy. He became so disenchanted with his new appointment and the suffocating protocol that he almost lost interest in his career.

It didn't last long. The battles with the Sikhs were getting fiercer, and the British troops under their existing officers were gaining no success; London was worried. Where was Sir Harry Smith? His hour was about to dawn. On 16 January 1846 Sir Hugh Gough sent for him and outlined the next campaign that was to drive more than ten thousand Sikhs back beyond the River Sutlej. To begin with, this would mean capturing the forts at Dharmkot and Fategarh.

The Sikhs, under their greatly respected leader Ranjur Singh, proved to be some of the toughest, cleverest opposition forces he had ever faced. This was now becoming a game of chess, each side trying to outwit the other. It was not until 28 January that Sir Harry showed who was the master. He remembered the words of Wellington: 'the business of war, as in life, is guessing what was at the other side of the hill.' But it helps if you can see something of that hill. So, with some of his cavalry, Sir Harry rode up to the highest village on the ridge and climbed to the top of a house. From there he saw a sight that made his heart thump with excitement – Ranjur Singh's army, which had grown to 18,000 men, with 67 guns, was set out in orderly formation waiting for the attack. Harry knew that his own well-disciplined brigades could muster only 12,000 men, and he was still uncertain of the ground between them.

Moving each of his brigades as carefully as chess-pieces he outmanoeuvred Singh; each thrust was carried out with such meticulous precision that it looked more like Trooping the Colour on Horse Guards Parade. When every piece was in place, Harry gave the orders for the final attack. The Sikh lines began to break and were eventually scattered. The British advance was now able to move forward at great speed. Sir Harry could be heard shouting above the noise of battle: 'Well done, 16th! You have covered yourselves with glory.' Ranjur Singh failed to regroup his men, and the Sikhs fled, leaving behind on the battlefield 3,000 dead and all their guns. Sir Harry's troops received more praise and an extra ration of grog.

Again, I have been forced to simplify this important event but, as Sir Harry himself was to write: 'Never was a victory more complete, and never was one fought under happier circumstances.' He knew that he had fought a great battle without making one error. The victory was made even more sweet for him when he heard that his hero, the Duke of Wellington, had paid tribute to him in the House of Lords, saying:

> I have read the accounts of many a battle, but I never read the account of one in which more ability, energy and experience have been manifested than this. I know of no one in which an officer ever showed himself more capable than this officer has in commanding troops in the field.

Compared with some of the previous battles, British losses were light. Out of the 12,000 men who went into battle 153 were killed, 413 wounded and 25 missing. One trooper who survived to tell of his part in this famous victory was a man named Eaton, who fought with the 16th Lancers, cheered on by Sir Harry. He remembered that Sir Harry addressed them all afterwards and said that they fought like devils, 'for you charged their ranks more like devils than anything else'. And then, said the trooper, we saw tears in the poor old man's eyes and he said, 'God bless you, my brave boys; I love you.'

You can imagine that when the news reached Whittlesey there was great pride and rejoicing, and the town was quick to name one of its pubs the *Hero of Aliwal* – long before it got round to naming a local school. Further honours were to pour in from cities, universities and civic societies throughout Britain, culminating – as if any further icing on the cake were needed – in a letter from the Prime Minister informing Harry that a baronetcy would be conferred upon him, to which he could append the word 'Aliwal' as a special distinction.

But even that is not the end of the story, though I hope you'll agree that I've said enough to explain why the Community College in our town bears the name of such an illustrious Smith. When the soldier himself returned to Whittlesey in June 1847 he received a rapturous reception. The streets were thronged with cheering people, estimated at ten thousand or more, which was considerably more than the town's population. There were civic and church dignitaries from all over the counties of Cambridgeshire, Norfolk, Lincolnshire and Northamptonshire. There were parades, speeches, dinners, more speeches, and demands to hear Sir Harry himself talk of his victory. He was deeply touched by such displays of affection and grateful to be back home. It is reported that when he walked past the house where he was born, and where his parents had always lived until their deaths, tears rolled down his cheeks, as they often did in emotional moments.

Home he may have been for a brief while, but it was not long before the Hero of Aliwal was on his travels overseas again, this time back to South Africa. In 1847 he was appointed Governor of the Cape of Good Hope and its dependencies, a province still far from the security of peace. On 24 September he and Lady Juana, set sail from Portsmouth in HMS *Vernon*. They arrived in Cape Town to another enthusiastic reception and, in stirring words from the steps of Government House, Harry declared to the people:

I am now the Governor, and I WILL BE THE GOVERNOR.

He was now sixty years old and beginning to look a weary man.

There were still many problems to solve, many political storms to settle in South Africa. But his influence, wisdom and example were to play an important part in the slow progress towards the kind of justice which he hoped one day would come. His forthright opinions and old cavalier attitude to authority did not please everyone, especially Lord Henry Grey, secretary of state for war and the colonies, known for his contempt of other people's opinions. He resented Smith's self-importance and persuaded the Government it was time to recall a man who was failing to show the energy and foresight his position required. Sir Harry, sadly, had had his day and he was brought home. Many of his friends saw this as nothing less than being given the sack, and there was much protest throughout the world at the way this national hero was treated.

Unfortunately, what most of his critics had failed to realize was that during his last year of service in South Africa his own brand of diplomacy and courage had averted what could have been a long and bloody racial war between the blacks and the whites, even between one black tribe and another. He did at least have the consolation of knowing that when he left that country an ugly and volatile situation had been calmed, and there was peace.

On 17 April 1852 Sir Harry and Lady Juana embarked on HMS *Gladiator* to sail back to England. Two years later Britain entered the Crimean War, but Harry was to have no part in that, even though he offered his services. His duties now were more those of a public-relations officer and morale-booster at home. It was not until seven years later, in September 1859, that he made his only surrender – to retirement. A year later, on 12 October 1860, he had a heart attack and died not far from his London home. His body was brought back to Whittlesey for burial. Twelve years later, on 10 October 1872, Juana died and was buried next to her husband in the town's new cemetery. The story was now complete.

There is now a memorial chapel dedicated to him in the parish church of St Mary's, just a few yards from the house where he was born, and, as you now know, a Community College and pub also bear his name. But can any monument do justice to such a strong, independent and courageous individual, one who could weep, swear, kill and love without reserve, and was known only to his Spanish wife as 'my loving Enrique'. It is doubtful if this country, let alone this town, will ever produce another such man to match his deeds.

❧ 4 ❧

Above the Gazing Multitudes

I have just spent three very pleasant days in Hampshire with some friends who, with some forethought, took me to the village of Selborne, where Gilbert White, the eighteenth-century naturalist, lived for most of his placid and patient life.

Now, you may be wondering what connection this has with a series of letters from the Fens. Let me assure you that there is one, and also that there are other reasons why I feel justified in telling you about my visit to another part of England. But, first of all, allow me to explain how I came to be interested in Gilbert White. If nothing else, it will illustrate again how beguilingly fate, or coincidence, pulls together such different threads into a recognizable pattern or weave.

As you know, I make no claims to being a naturalist, yet I have to admit that Gilbert White's now famous book *The Natural History of Selborne* (1788), always had a certain draw on my imagination. Perhaps it was because for several years I lived in a house called 'Selbourne' – spelt differently, as you can see, but with the same sound that came to have a familiar ring about it. Maybe it was my early interest in John Clare's writing that led me to look for other authors who had recorded their observations of birds, flowers, insects and trees with similar sensitivity and love.

Although he occasionally wrote verses, Gilbert White was not a poet, as Clare unquestionably was, but his love of the countryside was just as profound, as original and appealing. Apart from that, it would appear that the two men had little in common, even though Clare was later to read White with some enthusiasm. In a letter to his publisher John Taylor in April 1828, he quotes the Selborne naturalist: '"*Interest makes strange friendships*" White says, & I feel its truth & its misfortune.' I wonder. Had the two men been able to meet, would their interests have created such a strange friendship?

Gilbert White died in 1793, the year that Clare was born. He was the eldest son of a barrister and a grandson of another Gilbert White, who was the vicar of Selborne, where the younger Gilbert was born on 21 July 1720 – the same birthday month as Clare. The great difference was in their education. White received a good education, became a Fellow of Oriel College, Oxford, in 1744, then took Holy Orders, eventually becoming Junior Proctor of the University and Dean of his college. All a far cry from the formally uneducated Clare, which makes the crossing of their destinies all the more interesting to me.

In 1754 White became curate of Selborne, which meant he could return to his beloved home, known as The Wakes. It was from here that he began his correspondence with two acquaintances who were both interested in natural history – Thomas Pennant and Daines Barrington. It is largely due to these two scholars that Gilbert White finally agreed to his own studies being published, and only then because he persuaded his brother to read through all his papers, edit them and prepare them for publication in 1788. By then the collected letters and journals had grown into a history of the parish as well as one of the local flora and fauna.

It is indicative of this gentle man's character that he frequently declined preferment to more financially attractive parishes, so that he could devote himself to this daily study of his people and their customs, as well as the weather, his garden and the calendar of nature that obsessed him. His prose was plain and unaffected, and, unlike some clerical writers of that age, he did not indulge in purple passages or false sentiments.

One of the reasons why White appeals to me is that he was also a prolific letter-writer, and one letter was to make my visit to Selborne all the more interesting. It was not about birds, bees, bushes or flowers, but air-ballooning.

When I was writing *In Fen Country Heaven* (1996), I was surprised to discover that in the early eighteenth century the Parson Drove farmer John Peck had been an enthusiastic supporter of this latest wonder of the world – man's ability to fly. Although he never succeeded in getting a flight himself, he frequently travelled miles across the Fens to watch a balloon ascent. He was convinced that one day man would conquer the air so completely that flying would be commonplace. (His grandson, in fact, was to qualify, late in life, as a pilot out in Australia.)

Gilbert White at Selborne

But the sport – for that is what it was – was already nearly fifty years old by the time John Peck became interested in it. The first successes were in France with the Montgolfier brothers and Jean-François Pilâtre de Rozier who in 1783 proved to the world that flight was possible, that man could free himself from the shackles of the earth by riding in a basket suspended from a balloon filled with hydrogen. Soon there was to be a balloon mania. The first ascent in England was made on 15 September 1784 by Vincenzo Lunardi, though actually he was beaten by four weeks by a Scotsman, James Tytler, who constructed his own balloon and flew for half a mile from Comely Gardens, Edinburgh.

Lunardi's flight was more spectacular. He was at the time secretary to the Neapolitan Ambassador Prince Caramanico, and was so confident of his ascent being a great success that he wrote to King George III, inviting him to watch through a telescope as his 32-foot balloon took off from the Artillery Grounds, Moorfield. It was estimated that 200,000 people also gathered to witness the event, many believing it would end in disaster.

Vincenzo had a few hiccups to begin with, but eventually his balloon became airborne and sailed away. Writing later of the exhilaration he felt he said:

> My balloon ascended with a slow and majestic motion amidst the shouts and acclamations of a numberless multitude who liberally atoned for their suspicions of an impostor by their unbounded admiration and applause. At the height of twenty yards the globe was suddenly depressed by the wind, but on discharging a part of the ballast it ascended again and at the height of two hundred yards I repeated the salute of waving my flag, which I then threw down to convince such as were yet credulous that I still accompanied the balloon. . . . The stillness of the scene was inexpressibly awful; the prospect of London, with the surrounding countryside . . . presented a picture of which the liveliest fancy can form no idea.

This premier bird's-eye view lasted until Lunardi was forced to land at Ware. But the barrier had been broken. Man could fly like a bird – well, almost – and, unlike Icarus his wings would not melt by flying too near the sun.

Another Frenchman, M. Jean-Pierre Blanchard (who was the first man to cross the Channel by balloon in 1785), also gave demonstration flights in England. This, incredible though it may seem, brings me back to Gilbert White, who on 19 October 1784 wrote to his sister telling her of the feverish excitement in Selborne when it was known that M. Blanchard's balloon was expected to fly over their village within a day or two:

> I called on many of my neighbours in the street and told them of my suspicions ... exhorting all those who had any curiosity to look sharp from about one o' the clock to three towards London, as they would stand a good chance of being entertained with a very extraordinary sight. . . . I was not content to call at the houses only but went out to the plowmen and labourers in the fields. . . . At twenty minutes before three there was a cry in the street that the balloon was come. We ran into the orchard, where we found twenty or thirty neighbours assembled; and from the green bank at the S.W. end of my house saw a dark blue speck at a most prodigious height, dropping as it were from the sky and hanging amidst the regions of the upper air, between the weather-cock of the tower and the top of the maypole; but we soon discovered that its velocity was very considerable. . . . With a telescope I could discern the boat and the ropes that supported it. . . . I was wonderfully struck at first with the phenomenon; and, like Milton's 'belated peasant', felt my heart rebound with fear and joy at the same time.

Although hot-air-ballooning caught the public's imagination, not everyone approved. The Reverend John Newton (1725-1807), who was a friend of the poet William Cowper, thought that Mr Lunardi was tempting Providence. On 22 September 1784 he wrote:

> How great the hazard, how poor the motives. A strange creature man is, his powers of invention, the ardour and enterprise of his spirit bespeak his originality, but the misapplication of his powers loudly proclaim his depravity. He is continually making new discoveries, but to the need, and worth, and way of salvation, he is blind and insensible. . . . I fear this balloon mania will not subside till some awful events put a stop to it.

I seem to remember there were similar fears expressed about the first flight of Concorde and the first trip to the moon. And awful events there were, as there always will be in pioneering adventures. Many people were killed, including, in 1809, M. Blanchard himself. But the dream had become a reality. Soon regular flights were being

made across the English and Irish Channels and, one hundred years
later, flights of up to five hundred miles distance were being
achieved. In 1878 the largest balloon ever made was exhibited at
the Paris Exhibition. It contained 886,000 cubic feet of hydrogen
and could carry fifty passengers.

Just for interest's sake, fifty years earlier John Clare had also
recorded in his Journal the sighting of a balloon. On 2 July 1825 he
wrote:

> a balloon with Mr Green and Miss Stocks passed over our garden
> opposite the walnut tree.

Not only were the ladies taking up the sport as well, they were
also writing about it. Mary Alcock (1741-98), whose great-grandfather had been bishop of Peterborough in 1691, wrote a long
poem in which she extolled the thrills and freedom of ballooning:

> In Air Balloon to distant realms I go
> And leave the gazing multitude below.

But I am now getting out of my depth as well as height. I fear I
have digressed too long and must return to Selborne, if only to tell
you a little more about my day there. The house where Gilbert
White lived is now The Wakes Museum; which is really two museums in one. Half, naturally, is given over to the naturalist and the
other half is the Oates Memorial Museum. The latter commemo-
rates a nephew and his uncle: Captain Lawrence Oates (1880-1912),
the immortal companion of Captain Scott's heroic but ill-fated expe-
dition to the South Pole, and Frank Oates (1840-75), the ornitholo-
gist and explorer of Guatemala and Africa. Both museums are full of
unusual interest but my main concern was to follow the footsteps of
Gilbert White into each room of the house as he knew it: the Little
Parlour; the Great Parlour (which he added to the house in 1776/7);
the old kitchen, with its pots and pans; and his bed-chamber, where
he wrote most of *The Natural History of Selborne*.

In some ways one felt the presence of the man more in the large
garden, which he designed and helped to cultivate. Although it was
still early February when we were there, the day was bright and
golden in the afternoon light. Several spring flowers were in full
bloom, and most of the bushes in the shrubbery tipped with pink
new buds. The vast number of herb plants and rare trees would take

hours to name, but the garden's great virtue is its proximity to park-
land and Selborne Hanger, from where, for more than forty years,
White heard and noted an unending recital of bird-song.

Sadly, many of the songbirds about which both White and Clare
wrote as daily joys have now become so rare that they are hardly
ever heard or seen at all. During the last twenty-five years the population of some of those sublime singers has more than halved in this
country, especially of skylarks, thrushes and nightingales. Some will
soon disappear altogether, rather like the wild flowers that were
once common enough for children to pick freely and can now only
be found in picture-books.

But I must end with a real connection between Gilbert White and
the Fens. In a letter to Thomas Pennant, dated 2 January 1769, he
wrote:

> When I first saw Northamptonshire, Cambridgeshire, and the fens of
> Lincolnshire, I was amazed at the number of spires which presented
> themselves in every point of view. As an admirer of prospects I have
> reason to lament their want in my own country; for such objects are
> very necessary ingredients in an elegant landscape. . . . I have often
> thought that those vast extents of fens have never been sufficiently
> explored.

White was, of course, writing of the Fens only a century after
Cornelius Vermuyden had drained the Cambridgeshire Fens, and
much of Lincolnshire was still to be drained. Neither had the rich,
intensely-farmed land we know today, which has been quite sufficiently explored, if not exploited.

I learned also from White's Letters that he had indeed visited the
Fens as early as 1746, when he was invited to Spalding. Now why
was this quiet and unambitious naturalist from Hampshire invited
to Spalding? Was it to address the town's Gentlemen's Society,
which was started on an informal basis in 1710 and established as a
registered Society in 1712, or were there other reasons? I can't
imagine that his reputation at that time would have reached as far
as Lincolnshire, for his main work was still unpublished, but it will
be worth making a visit to Spalding one of these days to find out if
he attended one of their meetings as a guest.

The following day: I can't believe my luck. This morning I strolled
into a bookshop in Peterborough and bumped into an old friend

from Whittlesey – Betty Spridgeon, who was a Land Army girl in the Fens during the Second World War. She is a treasury of unusual snippets of information and knows the farms in the area very well. In the course of our conversation she mentioned Gilbert White. I think I should explain that Betty was in her wheelchair and the shop was extremely busy. 'Now don't tell me you know why and when he came to the Fens' I said. 'Well,' she said, 'it was to visit his uncle at Gores Farm, near Thorney. Didn't you know that?' I shook my head and asked if by any chance she knew which year. 'For all I know, he came more than once,' she replied from behind someone pushing between us, 'but I have just had a letter from a lady who is writing a book about Gilbert White, and she told me that he definitely came here in 1756 to sell the sheep, cattle and other effects when his uncle died. His uncle's name was Thomas Holt, and presumably Gilbert was his nearest relative if he had to come here to wind up the estate. I know the farm well, and so must you. It's on the left-hand side of the road as you come from Whittlesey to Thorney Dyke.'

We were clearly getting in the way of the other shoppers, so I thanked Betty for what she had told me and asked her to let me have anything else she was able to ferret out during the next few weeks. I was now excited to know that White's connections with the Fens were even closer than I had imagined.

Moments like this certainly put a sparkle in the day!

᪗ 5 ᪗

A Fenman's Reply to the Queen

A couple of Sunday mornings ago I woke early and switched on the radio. What I heard was a piece of unaccompanied choral music which instantly appealed to me. It set the mood for the day – peaceful and reassuring, an antidote to the new menace of Sunday trading which has made this day of rest as noisy as ordinary work-days. But who had written this calming music? Was it by Thomas Tallis, or William Byrd? Despite my limited knowledge of the subject, I felt sure it was of that period, and that it was also English. Then the announcer told me it was by Christopher Tye. And who was he? I asked myself.

I did not leap out of bed immediately to find out, but listened instead to the news headlines. I wished I had not; each item was again of some horror, bomb outrage, murder or political sleaze. So, before the effect of that gentle awaking was completely ruined by also listening to the weather forecast, I turned off the radio and went downstairs to make a cup of tea.

A few moments later I was searching through some of my music reference books and was delighted, amazed, even amused to discover that Christopher Tye had once been the vicar of the Fenland parish known at the time as Doddington-cum-March. I smiled even more to think that the now bigger, thriving town of March was once tacked on to the humbler Doddington, but such are the whims of history.

Delving into a few more pages I learned that, before taking holy orders, Christopher Tye had been organist at Ely Cathedral and, before that, a chorister at King's College Chapel, Cambridge. In his latter years he was also a Gentleman at the Chapel Royal, Windsor, where he upset Elizabeth I.

It is not very often that one stumbles across an intriguing story

41

like this in the Fens, so I knew that whatever I had planned for the day would now have to take second place. It did not take long to find there was a scarcity of information, and that much of what is known about Tye has been arrived at through speculation. The musicologists were uncertain about the date of his birth, though most agreed that he was probably born in the Isle of Ely sometime between 1501 and 1503 and that he died around 1572-73. We do know, however, that he served four monarchs and was to be highly regarded as a friend by the young Edward VI, the only legitimate son of Henry VIII. It was a brief friendship, for Edward died in 1553 at the age of fifteen. We learn something of Christopher Tye's reputation and standing at court from Samuel Rowley's play *When You See Me, You Know Me*, which was first performed in 1613. In one scene the dramatist has Prince Edward addressing Tye with:

> Doctor, I thank you and commend your cunning;
> I oft have heard my father merrily speak
> In your high praise, and this his highness saith -
> 'England one God, one Truth, one Doctor hath
> For music's art, and that is Doctor Tye,
> Admired for his skill in music's harmony.'

I suppose what surprised me most was not that Dr Tye had once been so popular at court but that he had ever lived at Doddington. I have known this village on and off for most of my life. When I was a child, and my father played in one of the local brass bands, I remember that a special day of the year for the town was Hospital Sunday – which, because of the way it was pronounced by the townspeople, always sounded like 'horse-piddle Sunday', creating some confusion in my young mind. It was, however, the day when the band gave a concert in the large, park-like gardens of a prominent solicitor to raise money for the two neighbouring hospitals – Peterborough and/or Doddington. As a young man I had been a patient in the latter, and it was also where both my parents were to spend some of their last days. So Doddington was not a place for which I held a great deal of affection, and it has always been one that I have hurried through on my way to somewhere else.

But now I had a reason to give it more time and to take a closer look at its history. Doddington was at one time the largest parish in the county, with close on 40,000 acres, and it owned the wealthiest living in the kingdom. The rectory was so grand it was frequently

Doddington Parish Church

used as a palace for the Bishops of Ely and also to entertain distinguished visitors to the diocese, both from the church and the royal
court. It is still an impressive building, but no longer a suitable or
economic dwelling for today's more modest incumbents.

The day that I drove over to Doddington was one of those wild
and windy days that one often gets in the Fens during late March.
Stormy clouds were stampeding across the sky, and the leaning telegraph poles looked as frail as corn-stalks as they strained to stay
upright. I glanced briefly at the nearby hospital buildings then made
my way to the church. As I expected, it was locked, and I could not
find a notice telling me where I might obtain a key, so I walked
round the churchyard, which had an interesting collection of nineteenth-century headstones and a few crumbling ones of an earlier
date. They stood, leaning shoulder-to-shoulder in a sad stance of
defiance, but to no end – their inscriptions were, as Thomas Hardy

would have said, 'in years defaced and lost', for time and the
weather had eaten away each brief biography. Yet the grass was well
kept and had just been cut. Many of the more recent graves in the
newer cemetery were decorated with primroses or daffodils, and it
was obvious that the people of Doddington cared about the place.
Only the protesting rooks in the surrounding trees seemed to take
exception to my presence, or maybe they were simply arguing
amongst themselves over which branches they wanted for their
nest-building.

I leaned for a few moments against one of the old tombstones
and looked at the church which had seen a few changes since Dr Tye
preached there. Nevertheless, there it was, and this chapter of its
history was all new to me. How little one knows of one's own
county, I thought. I consoled myself with the knowledge that I was
not alone in being ignorant of its once famous priest and composer.

One of the reasons why there has been some confusion over
Christopher Tye's actual dates is because there was also a Robert
Tye, who was a chorister and then lay clerk at King's College
Chapel in 1528 – by which time Christopher would have graduated
from being a treble to a senior member of the choir. Some dates,
however, do fit into a margin of common agreement. We know that
in 1536 he took his Mus. B. at Cambridge, and that he became
organist at Ely Cathedral during that year. Six years later he
accepted the appointment of Master of Choristers for a salary of
£10 a year and was responsible for all the cathedral's music. By the
time a further two years had passed he had become a Doctor of
Music and was establishing his reputation as a composer of both
sacred and secular music. He provided several masses for Henry
VIII, motets for Edward VI, consort music for Mary Tudor, and
Services for Queen Elizabeth. He was, by later musicians, to be
considered the father of the English anthem and composed several
hymn tunes which, in various arrangements, are still popular today.

It would seem that the course of his career was firmly set, but in
1560 Dr Tye decided to take holy orders, and in 1561 he resigned
from his musical offices at Ely Cathedral. He did so knowing that
he would be offered a lucrative living which would also allow his
music to prosper. He was succeeded at Ely in 1562 by another
Cambridge scholar, Robert White (1535-74), who subsequently
married Tye's daughter Ellen. Eight years later White went on to
become Master of the Choristers at Westminster Abbey but, at the
age of 39 died of the plague. Again, who would have thought such

illustrious ambitions and achievements were being realized out there in the Fens four hundred years ago.

Dr Tye's ambitions appeared to have no end. In addition to getting one of the richest livings in the land at Doddington-cum-March, he also acquired two smaller ones in 1564 – Wilbraham Parva and Newton-cum-Capella. Alas, it soon became clear that they were too much for his limited pastoral and administrative skills, for they were soon sequestered: not only had he neglected them as a priest, he had also failed to pay 'the first fruits' to the Crown. He was not alone; his bishop was to receive a royal rap over the knuckles from Queen Elizabeth for showing his reluctance in handing over Ely manor at her demands:

> Proud prelate, I understand you are backward in complying with your agreement but I would have you know, that I, who made you what you are, can unmake you and if you do not forthwith fulfil your engagement, I will unfrock you.
>
> ELIZABETH R.

A few years later Tye himself was to be reprimanded by the Queen when he was organist at the Chapel Royal. Anthony Wood, the seventeenth-century historian, wrote of him that he was:

> a peevish and humoursome man, especially in his latter days, and sometimes, playing on ye organ in ye chappell of Queen Elizabeth, which contained much music but little to delight her ear, she would send ye verger to tell him that he played out of tune; whereupon he sent word back to say that it was her ears that were out of tune.

One can only assume that Dr Tye felt sufficiently safe in his musical reputation to reply to her majesty in this brusque way – or that, as a Fenman, he didn't really give a damn what she thought of him or his music.

As far as we know he returned unharmed and unrepentant to his wife Katharine and family at Doddington, where he was able to concentrate on his composing, the writing of verses and his music-making. He was a skilled exponent of the viol, could play all keyboard instruments and loved singing. He invited many of his musical friends to stay with him at the rectory, establishing what, in Schubert's day, came to be known as Schubertiads (it is not as easy to coin a word on the name Tye). Then, as so often happens after a person's death, his reputation declined, and much of his music was lost or forgotten until our own time. What would he say now, I wonder, if he could see, and hear, the number of CD recordings of his compositions that are currently available? Still, I suppose we could say the same thing about Schubert himself, or Mozart.

You must be aware by now that, once my interest is aroused in something I knew nothing about, I do not rest easily until I have tried to remedy my ignorance. Since that Sunday morning of two weeks ago I have been phoning, or writing to, some of my musical friends to see if they could tell me more about Christopher Tye. The most satisfying response came from someone I have known for a long time – Barry Ferguson, who, apart from taking holy orders, has had a career not dissimilar to that of Dr Tye. He too was at Cambridge, where he studied with Sir David Willcocks, then became assistant organist at Peterborough during what he calls 'the vintage years of Dr Stanley Vann'. Later he moved to Wimborne Minster and eventually to Rochester Cathedral as Organist and Master of the Choristers. He has also composed a considerable amount of choral music and song-cycles, and is now a freelance composer, accompanist and lecturer. Included in his letter were a few paragraphs from a book by one of his former tutors – Peter Le Huray, who wrote in his *Music and the Reformation in England* (Herbert Jenkins 1967), that Christopher Tye's music 'delighted in rich sonorities' and was of 'considerable importance, for it covers a particularly wide range of styles and techniques'. He concluded his brief essay by saying 'his music deserves wider recognition'.

All this, I trust, justifies my recent passion and, who knows, by writing to you about it I might even help a little to bring about that recognition, for it would be a pity for this composer to remain in the shadows of his more illustrious contemporaries any longer.

But one mystery remains. Where was Christopher Tye buried? It is fairly certain that he stayed at Doddington until his death, because his successor was appointed within a year. Perhaps someone will come up with the answer one day, and I shall be able to set off on another pilgrimage. I am already more than grateful that one Sunday morning I discovered his music by accident and have since been able to extend my knowledge of it by buying some of the recordings. For all I know, Dr Tye may not have received one single inspiration from the Fens, but when I drive across that landscape now, it is his music I hear in the air, and my heart is made lighter because of his genius.

Now, should you be thinking that you have never heard a note of his music, let me assure you that you have. We all have. For one tune alone has given him immortality. The next time you sing 'While Shepherds Watched Their Flocks by Night', spare a thought for the vicar of Doddington, the Fenland composer who dared to tell the Queen that her ears were out of tune, for they will be his notes that were adapted for this well-known carol we annually huff into the frosty air as we prepare for Christmas.

Finally, in fairness to the rest of the Isle of Ely, I should mention that Dr Tye was not the only composer to be associated with the Cambridgeshire Fens. Some 250 years later George Guest (who was born in Bury St Edmunds in 1771) was appointed organist at St Peter's Church, Wisbech, where he stayed for 42 years. During this time he composed a vast amount of church music, including enough hymn tunes to publish his own hymn-book in 1820. He was also greatly admired as a pianist, teacher and organist. An entry in a *Dictionary of Music* (1824) tells us that 'Mr Guest has long excited great admiration by the correctness and elegance with which he pours forth the impulses of the moment; to a thorough knowledge of his art and a complete command of the instrument is added the excellence of a chaste yet brilliant conception of musical ideas.' He may not have reached the heights attained by Christopher Tye, but I hope you will agree that he, too, does not deserve to be forgotten.

I shall be writing to you about other Wisbech celebrities in a few weeks' time but now I feel it might be more appropriate to put on some of the music that was written at Doddington more than five hundred years ago. I can assure you it is therapeutic if nothing else.

☙ 6 ❧

Another World Beyond a Front Door

You will remember two letters ago I said that one day I would go to Spalding to see if I could find out whether Gilbert White had ever been a guest at the Gentlemen's Society when he visited the town in 1746. Although I have now found out why he did occasionally come to the Fens, if only to see to his uncle's affairs ten years later, I still thought it worth making a few inquiries in Spalding. And, in any case, I do want to write a letter to you about that prestigious Society which has its own lengthy history.

Because it was such a brand-new-looking day I decided to go by train, so that I could appreciate the countryside rather than stare continually at those monotonous white lines on busy roads. Driving a car and trying to take in all the subtleties of a landscape are two activities that do not go well together; past attempts have not endeared me to other motorists.

Soon I was being beguiled by the acres of rape which had already taken over the yellow of earlier daffodil crops. The immaculately harrowed soil of unsown fields looked more like brushed suede, despite the land's desperate thirst for rain. Some of the new wheat appeared to contradict the threat of drought, for it was a vivid green, and most of the hedges were in flower. In the distance I saw the unmistakable silhouette of Crowland Abbey and, every now and again, the glistening water in the dykes lured my eyes to the far-off horizon. The sky looked skin-tight and translucent. How could I possibly have enjoyed all these delights from a car? At one stage a pheasant took off from the grass verge by the side of the line and decided to have a race with the one-carriage train. He almost won.

In fact I was a little worried to see that we were running sixteen minutes later than scheduled and wondered whether I would get to my appointment on time. Fortunately it was only a short sprint from the station to the town centre, and, a little breathless from the effort, I rang the door-bell punctually at ten-thirty.

One rarely knows what lies beyond a front door until one steps inside. Even expectations can fall embarrassingly short of reality. Such was my experience when I was invited into the headquarters and museum of the Spalding Gentlemen's Society to meet its current President, Mr Norman Leveritt, who has been a member for thirty-eight years.

But, you may be asking, what exactly is a Gentlemen's Society these days? Well, I can assure you of at least one thing: it is not as stuffy, archaic, bigoted or elitist as it might sound to modern ears. It is a society of men from all walks of life (and now from all parts of the world), who have shared in the common pursuit of knowledge, not for academic achievement or personal acclaim, but for the enrichment of life, for themselves and the people with whom they have lived and worked. The Society's interests range from the natural sciences to antiques, from classical civilization to architecture, from law to literature. I was to learn later that no subject was barred, except the controversial ones of religion and politics. How wise!

Having stepped beyond the front door I was ushered into the inner sanctum by Mr. J.W. Belsham the Honorary Curator. After being introduced to Mr Leveritt I was asked to make myself comfortable in an old leather armchair. But it was not easy to sit still in an elegant room full of lovely furniture and tall cases displaying unusual artefacts, so I was soon on my feet asking questions and not wanting to waste a second.

I was immediately aware that both Mr Leveritt and Mr Belsham have a deep affection for, and a pride in, their Society's unbroken history of nearly three hundred years – which, by any standard, is an outstanding record. Apart from the Royal Society in London, the Spalding Gentlemen's Society is the oldest in the country. Its membership today stands at over three hundred and includes scholars from many countries who are researching particular aspects of our history, knowing that the answers they seek may well be found in the archives at Spalding.

Again, you may be wondering how such an established Society should come to exist in this Fenland town, which is more famous for its Tulip Festivals. In one sense the answer is simple; it was started in 1710 by a young local barrister, Mr Maurice Johnson, who was born in 1688 and died in 1755. What is not so easy to explain is how the Society survived and is still thriving as we approach the millennium. To give a satisfactory answer to that question would mean writing a full account of its activities over nearly three centuries.

In case you still have the impression that the Society is more like a gentlemen's club, with retired old fuddy-duddies slumped in armchairs and taking all day to read a newspaper, let me remind you that its founder was only twenty-one when he decided to invite a few local people to a series of informal meetings at a coffee-house in the Abbey Yard, where they could discuss the sciences, arts, antiques, architecture and history. Maurice Johnson was himself an acknowledged antiquary and was to play a leading part in the refounding of the Society of Antiquaries of London, which meant the Spalding and London Societies could enjoy the mutual exchange of minutes, papers and ideas for their meetings. In the early days the Spalding men had relied on the new and often controversial journal *The Tatler* to fuel their opinions, but soon their sources of information were to cover a much wider field.

In 1712, after two years of informal meetings, it was agreed that the Society should establish itself on a more permanent and official basis by inviting membership and subscription. There was one novel stipulation, which I think could have been copied by other societies, and that was that each new member had to donate a book to the library. Consequently, over the years, the Spalding Society has accumulated a magnificent collection of books, some of them now very rare. When I was later shown round the library I was overwhelmed by its eclectic content and more than impressed by the efforts of its members to preserve their inheritance. After so many years of use

Books: a token of membership

some of the oldest books inevitably need repairing. A costly rebinding programme is just one of the Society's responsibilities, but it is being carried out with thoughtfulness and diligence.

The President impressed upon me again that the aims of the Society were not narrow or exclusive in any way. Its members were more than a cosy group of antiquarians, more than the casual keepers of an unusual museum, or the custodians of a private library. The Society existed now for the same reason that had inspired its founder nearly three hundred years ago: to promote knowledge and to extend learning within the community. It is, if you like, a debating society with a difference, perpetuating its own long history. In the early days it must have been the most progressive society in the provinces.

Among some of the Society's first members were distinguished people like Sir Isaac Newton, Alexander Pope, John Gay, Samuel Wesley and the Lord Mayor of London. Later members were to include Alfred, Lord Tennyson, Sir Gilbert Scott and Lord Coleraine. I noticed that one of the lecturers in recent years was the popular television expert on antiques Arthur Negus.

The present museum was opened in 1911 when the Society moved to its new premises in Broad Street. The erection of this fine building was made possible by the generous donations of members and a bicentenary appeal. The carved panels on the outside were done by a Belgian refugee, Jules Tuernlinckx of Mechelen (Malines), who was exiled in Spalding during the First World War.

With time already passing far too quickly, Norman Leveritt suggested I should take a look in the strong-room, an impressive chamber guarded by a door heavy enough to protect the Crown Jewels. There I was shown the very first Minute Books of 1712, some in Maurice Johnson's own elegant handwriting; then some copies of the Stamford radical newspaper *The Bee*, which had published some of John Clare's early poems; there too was the Wrest Park Cartulary of Croyland Abbey, written in the reigns of Edward III, Richard II and Henry IV. Elsewhere in the museum I was able to brush my fingers reverently over a framed manuscript of a poem by Tennyson, complete with doodles, and see examples of the straw-plaiting done by the French prisoners-of-war at Norman Cross during the Napoleonic Wars. There were displays of porcelain, silver, glass, armoury, jade, costumes and paintings, and a very rare tapestry depicting the head of Christ, done by Jas

Christopher le Blon and presented to the museum by Sir Richard Manningham in 1732. Room after room was full of revelation and delight. I now had no difficulty in understanding why this Society has thrived for so long, nor why its large lecture-room is filled meeting after meeting with its dedicated members.

Candidates for membership must be personally known to the members who sponsor them, and their applications have to be seconded by three other members. Election is then by a ballot of the Council of the Society. At the time of writing the oldest member is in his mid-nineties and has belonged to the Society for seventy years.

Inevitably, in such a long established institution, there are some quaint and endearing customs. The one that appealed to me concerned the Society's poker. I had noticed in one of the early Minute Books an item which referred to the cost of repairing a poker. Why was that so important, I wondered. Norman Leveritt explained that traditionally the poker was always kept on the right-hand side of the hearth and only the President was allowed to use it to stir the fire, holding it in his right hand, of course!

This rather scanty summary has done no more than outline some of the achievements of this ancient and worthy Society, but, as I said at the beginning of this letter, 'one very rarely knows what lies beyond a front door until one steps inside'. My morning there had proved to be all too brief to take in all the President and Curator wanted to show me. If true knowledge is a quest for what will enrich our lives in the fullest sense, then I can only think of the Gentlemen's Society in Broad Street as a treasure-house of the best of what earlier generations have left for the present and the future to enjoy.

You can imagine that it was something of a shock to step outside again into the brash and noisy reality of our own times. In my haste to get to the station I collided first of all with a wayward trolley from a supermarket and was then nearly crippled for my old age by an empty push-chair propelled by a madwoman who took an instant dislike to me. I was tempted to rush back to the museum to see if they would take me in, offer me a refuge in an age when things like this didn't happen. (Or did they? Each age knows its own violence and lack of civility. When I am reading through old newspapers or parish magazines it is revealing to see reports of muggings, robberies and vandalism which we have assumed to be the social evils inflicted solely on the twentieth century.)

Those two minor incidents, however, could in no way tarnish the day; in retrospect they rather amuse. By the time the one-carriage train slithered out of the station, dead on time, and shuttled me back across the shining Fens, I was able to relax, to appreciate my good fortune at being able to do the journey in a fraction of the time it would have taken three hundred years earlier. There was even a touching moment at the end when the guard said over the public-address system: 'This is your senior guard speaking. We are now approaching Peterborough where this train will terminate. Please make sure you've got your baggage with you and thank you for travelling with . . .' – and here he forgot the name of his new privatized company. 'Ah well!' he said, 'It's all the same. Mind how you go, and God bless!' It was a genuine impromptu that made the other four passengers smile, and did indeed put a blessing on the day. I may not have found out why Gilbert White went to Spalding in 1746, but I do know why I went in 1997. Behind that front door in Broad Street was another world – one which I hope I shall have the privilege of visiting again before I reach the millennium.

And as if all that wasn't enough, the day dispensed an added bonus in the afternoon, demonstrating again how so many strands in the web are brought together for our delight. I was looking through some papers borrowed from my friend Dr Peter Cave of Wisbech and came across his notes on Dr Richard Middleton Massey (1678-1743) who was an eminent physician and disciple of Sir Hans Sloane, both early members of the Spalding Gentlemen's Society. Massey was to spend twenty-two years of his life in the Fens, and I hope to be writing more about him later. I mention him now because in Peter's notes there was an extract from the Society's house rules to which members must adhere:

> they must meet at Four when the season requires; there must be a good fire during the meetings . . . a Pot of Coffee & a Pot of Bohea Tea . . . twelve clean Pipes and an ounce of best Tobacco . . . a Chamber Pot . . . a Latin Dictionary & a Greek Lexicon . . . and all the printed Papers ordered by the Society. . . . The Coffee & Tea must be ready exactly at Five and taken away before Six, which done, the Papers must be read by some Members. Then a tankard of ale holding one Quart and No More must be set upon the Table. The President shall always sit on the Right side of the Chimney and take care of the Fire.

Which brings us back to Norman Leveritt's story of the poker. And that, I submit, is as good an example of tradition as you can get.

Notes from the Parish

The longer I live the more certain I am of the old saying that there is nothing new under the sun. Did you know, for instance, that man had actually landed on the moon more than three hundred years before the Americans or Russians had even thought of it? Well, that is what I read the other day in an encyclopaedia of general knowledge.

It appears that in 1640 a Bishop Godwin wrote of a voyage to the moon by a Spanish nobleman in a spaceship pulled by twenty-five swans. He explained how, forty-five miles up, this first astronaut became weightless and saw the earth rotating like another star. It took twelve days to get there and, when he did, he found the people most friendly and about twenty-eight feet tall. He sat down with them in their gardens, talking of faraway places like London, Paris, Madrid and Rome. But they would not believe that such backward cities still existed on earth so late in the century.

How extraordinary, I thought. Then I remembered something my grandfather often said, which was that he had never known paper to refuse ink. So I took this amusing story with a pinch of salt whilst giving the seventeenth-century bishop credit for knowing about weightlessness in space. And then I thought, how can we be sure that what we are being told today is any more true and trustworthy? I have met more than one Fenman who still does not believe that men have been to the moon, and must admit that I do not know how to answer them when they say 'but 'ev yew got proof?'. There are times, too, when I feel it is a pity we can't find twenty-five swans to take us away from a world that is still often backward and fear-ridden.

But – to come back to earth, and a little nearer our own time – I am frequently surprised at how even the smallest affairs in our history are repeated, especially at parish level. We may think we are initiating some wonderful scheme for the improvement of society but it's odds-on that the idea has been thought of before, if not carried out.

A few weeks ago I attended the first annual general meeting of the Friends of St Mary's Church, Whittlesey, which was formed in January 1996 to discuss ways of raising money for the urgent repairs needed on that fine, historic building. It was estimated that something like £100,000 would have to be found from somewhere if the church was to be made safe for use, and its elegant spire to remain a significant landmark in the Fens. It was decided that everyone connected with the town should be made aware of the seriousness of the problem, and that as many events as possible be organized to help swell the funds. These were noble aims put forward by enthusiastic people who cared about their parish church.

The reason why I mention this is because I have just been 'trawling' – I think that is the correct jargon these days – through some old parish magazines. And what did I find? In 1886 it was reported:

> The upper part of the beautiful spire of St Mary's church has been undergoing urgent repairs during the past fortnight. It is believed that the spire was struck by lightning, although twenty-seven years ago a new conductor was erected. The second stone from the top was found to be completely split through, and it was wisely resolved by those in authority to replace the damaged stone by a new one. A considerable expense will be incurred but it will, without doubt, soon be met, for the people in the district are most willing to assist in keeping in repair so splendid a piece of architecture of which they are justly proud.

The words of that last sentence must be encouraging to the committee of the new Friends.

Later in the year, that earlier parish correspondent was able to announce that the work had been satisfactorily completed, though not without a few problems:

> After the necessary scaffolding had been erected and the damaged stones renewed, the work was delayed for several days in consequence of very rough, stormy weather, which must have subjected the beautifully tapering spire (nearly 200 ft high) to a very severe and unusual strain. Soon as weather permitted, the work was proceeded

with and finished, the large weather-vane re-gilded, and the spire repointed for about 30 feet downwards. As before stated, it was believed to have been struck by lightning years ago, but though this could not be positively asserted, yet the Sun Insurance Company, in which the edifice is insured, upon being applied to, promptly responded with a donation of £25 towards expenses.

The persuasive correspondent also added:

> We can hardly conceive that so beautiful a church will be allowed by the inhabitants of this town to sustain serious and permanent injury.

Those sentiments, I'm sure, are as true today as they were over one hundred years ago, and the Friends of St Mary's have accepted the challenge with a willingness and good humour that deserve success.

Before moving on to other titbits let me tell you of another joy I derived from attending that annual general meeting. After the business matters had been efficiently dealt with by the Chairman, Mr Gordon Ryall, we had an entertaining talk by Major Christopher Robinson, the great-great nephew of none other than Whittlesey's most popular hero Sir Harry Smith. It was as if the years had been rolled back, and the great man himself stood there with his medals, his amusing anecdotes, and a twinkle in his eye. The Peninsular War, Lady Juana, the Battle of Aliwal and South Africa all came to life on that Saturday afternoon when the wind buffeted the church, putting the spire again under 'a very severe and unusual strain'.

A totally different problem, and one which we sometimes believe to be unique to the late twentieth century, is vandalism. Hardly an hour goes by without we hear on the radio, or read in the newspapers, of some piece of public property that has been mindlessly damaged by youths who claim they are bored. It was, nevertheless, a nuisance not entirely unknown to our forefathers. In June 1886 the parish magazine published a reassurance to the inhabitants of Whittlesey that 'the state of affairs in St Mary's churchyard will, in all probability, soon be greatly improved'. It went on to say:

> The Burial Board have taken the matter in hand and will do their best to prevent the desecration to which it has so long been subjected. . . . There are two public pathways through it which cannot be stopped. These it is proposed to rail off from being made a playground and the rendezvous of the idle and dissolute.

Now I know that in my youth there were quite a few people who were known to be both, and, for some peculiar reason, churchyards were very popular among the courting couples of that time. But in 1886? It just goes to prove, if ever proof were needed, that human nature changes little, and that what happens in our parishes is simply a microcosm of life everywhere. In the parish magazine for Yaxley, September 1891, it was reported that the grapes and other produce from the harvest festival could not be given to the poor that year as some youths had broken into the church and stolen most of it. Similarly, in the little village of Manea street lamps were lit for the first time in January 1886 which were to prove 'a great boon to the inhabitants, especially on those dark Sunday nights which prove such a temptation to the youth of Manea – we regret to say of both sexes – who are extremely noisy and rude'.

But let me return for a moment to the subject of burial-grounds and funerals, mainly because I found a curious entry about an unusual request made in 1733:

> Mr John Underwood, of Whittlesey, Cambridgeshire, left £6,000 to his sister on condition of her carrying out his wishes respecting his funeral, and the lady wisely sacrificed her feelings rather than her fortune, and fulfilled his last injunctions to the letter. The dead man was placed in a green coffin, clad in his usual every day dress. His head resting on Saradon's *Horace*; Bentley's edition being placed under him and the same editor's edition of *Milton* lying at his feet. The right hand of the corpse clasped a small Greek Testament, while the left grasped a miniature edition of *Horace*. No bell was tolled, but after the Burial Service had been read, an arch was turned over the coffin and a piece of marble placed in the centre, inscribed 'Non omnis moriar, 1733.' The six mourners, or the gentlemen who did duty as such, then sang the last stanza of the Ode in which Horace deprecates any display of grief for the dead. Adjourning to their dead friend's house, the six sat down to an excellent supper. As soon as the cloth was removed, they performed a requiem in the shape of another Horatical Ode; and, after making themselves merry with a cheerful glass, departed to their several houses, and we suppose fulfilled the testator's final injunction to –
>
> THINK NO MORE OF JOHN UNDERWOOD.

Whittlesey has always had its share of characters but here is one I would like to think more of and to know more about. Obviously he was a man of means and a scholar, and had a mind of his own.

Another topic which claimed a fair bit of space in those early parish magazines was the Sunday School Treat, a nineteenth-century institution that today's children would find very dull, comical, and down-market. Most of these annual 'treats' started with a service, including a sermon, and the children must have wondered if they were ever going to get to the trestle tables loaded with bread and butter, cakes, scones and trifle. After tea there were more speeches of thanks and then organized games. Finally, 'the National Anthem having been sung, a bun was presented to each child upon leaving the field, thus bringing to a pleasant end a most enjoyable occasion'.

It all sounds rather quaint now, doesn't it? But in those precarious years just before the Second World War I can remember Sunday School Treats that were very similar, when all the Sunday Schools were brought together for what was meant to be a day of fun. Sometimes this even got as far as taking us to the seaside for the day, and more than one little Christian ended up with a bloody nose for stealing someone else's bucket and spade, or for trampling down a neighbour's sandcastle. What I do not remember surviving into our childhood are some of the games played by those earlier children, such as 'Jimmy', 'Basket and Pole Dodge', 'How Do You Like Your Neighbour?' and 'Earth, Air and Water', which was, I think, a game of forfeits. If they mean anything to you perhaps you would let me know.

Before putting these parish magazines back on the shelves to gather a little more dust, there is just one more entry that I would like to mention, if only to illustrate again how we deceive ourselves into believing that nothing beneficial or constructive happened in our communities before 1940, such as adult education. We may smile now at the simplicity of it all, but at least the vision and earnestness were there to improve the educational opportunities of those who had to leave school at fourteen, or earlier. This report comes from the village of Benwick in 1885:

EVENING SCHOOL: Mr Henry King, the Master of the Board Schools, wound up the Evening School season last week by giving all the scholars a very excellent tea, and a magic lantern entertainment afterwards. Upwards of 50 people were entertained at tea and a number of the older children in the Day School were admitted afterwards to see the Magic Lantern show. The slides, representing discoveries in the Arctic Regions, were interesting and instructive. There were also a number of comic pictures, which highly delighted the younger ones. . . . Mr King has had a good Night School this winter with 43 on the books, and almost that number were presented to the Inspector of Education.

Yes, things have changed, especially in education, and it is difficult to believe that evening classes were looked upon by some local councillors as a luxury and burden on the rates. Stories abound about the philistine attitudes taken by civic elders, even after the war. One old French tutor I knew assured me that when he started his evening classes in 1947 his students had to take candles with them, because the local authority would only pay for the hire of the schoolroom, not the lighting. Nor would they have paid for the heating, had there been any; consequently the students kept their overcoats and scarves on whilst trying to learn a new language. I even heard of a life-drawing class where the model insisted on wearing her fur coat, giving the students only an occasional glimpse of what lay hidden underneath – which created a situation far more erotic than it was meant to be. When I eventually went to work in adult education I was shocked by the penny-pinching mentality of the finance committees who could spend hours discussing whether or not to spend six shillings on a new stapler or half-a-crown on a box of paper-clips. Now, I suppose, they argue over language laboratories and computer rooms.

I will end these rambling parish notes by telling you of a really delightful evening I had last week when I was asked to give a talk to a group of retired people who wanted to know something more about the Fens. There is a magical quality about driving across the Fens on an early April evening that is difficult to surpass. The land has a nascent look about it, as if everything is at that point of beginning where all appears new and strange at first, unspoilt by men or the elements – though both have made the scene what it is. Under the immense light of a cloudless sky the land seemed even flatter than usual. Telegraph poles, scattered at random across the fields, looked like the pins on a bagatelle table, and the sun reverberated like an oriental gong whose sound had long been sucked into space.

Such satisfying sights always put me in a good humour, and I think I gave my audience a talk to match my mood. Even so, I was not prepared for one or two of the questions that followed. For instance, would I have been as interested in the Fens if I had not been a writer? Possibly not, I replied. (But what might have been an equally probing question is whether I would have become a writer at all if I had not been born in the Fens.) The next question was even more disarming. How, or why, do I keep on writing about the same dull, flat, uninteresting landscape with such undiminished enthusiasm? I felt like saying that, if the question still needed to be asked, then all my books so far have been a dismal failure. Instead I tried to explain what the landscape meant to me, and how it fed my imagination.

I suppose it would be true to say that half the time I am really writing about a personal landscape, about *my* world, rather than an actual geographical area that any historian could write about. I am not an historian, nor am I a geographer. I do not write about the *land*, or explain why the fields are laid out in the way that they are, or for what purpose. I know very little about social economy or scientific farming. I try to evoke 'the spirit of place' and what that place does to me. The very word *landscape* can itself become abstract and mean several different things, depending on the aspect of topography or history being discussed. I am fairly certain that for many people a particular place, with all its personal associations – family, work, hobbies, friends and interests – is embraced by the word *landscape*, which includes rivers, mists, sunrises, stars, furrows, snowfalls and summers. When I decided to become a writer it was inevitable that I should draw on my native landscape and, in doing so, use all its natural features as images in my work. Space, distance, light, the soil, farm-workers, and even such practical eyesores as pylons acquired a significance that almost made them symbolic. You know how an open window, or a hand-mirror held up in a crowd, can suddenly catch the sun and then flash such an intense light that it almost blinds you. Well, for me, the Fens are like that. Without warning, they can dazzle, amaze, beguile and even shock you into an awareness of something you have never experienced before.

The discussion went on for half an hour beyond our allotted time and was, I hope, enlightening to us all. When I left the hall to drive the thirty miles back home it was, of course, dark, and my attitude to the surrounding fields much more cautious. Fortunately a jaffa-orange moon put a bloom on the earth that made it look even more mysterious and beautiful, and I felt no great urgency to hurry towards the artificial lights of what we believe is civilization. Eventually I came to a railway crossing on the main line from

London to the North. The red barrier lights were flashing, and I slowed down to wait for the train to pass through. I could already see it approaching in the distance – a sleek express with its rows of lighted windows, looking more like an illuminated zip-fastener pulling the velvet sky and earth together. When it had passed the Fens felt even more silent and empty.

✺ 8 ✺

Home and Away

I have been kissed by some peculiar things in my time, including people, but not until that early April Sunday had I been kissed by a llama.

Where on earth, you might ask, did I find a llama in the Fens? For all I know there could be one or two munching somewhere around as Fenland farmers seek to diversify their stock, but I have never seen them.

No, the one with whom I became intimate, or perhaps it would be more accurate to say the one who became intimate with me, was on the other side of the country – on the borders of Shropshire and Wales.

The reason why my wife and I were so far from home is because we had gone to visit two friends, the poet Roger Garfitt and his wife Margaret, who is a librarian. I had first met Roger when he was on a visit to the Fens, accompanying a group of students from Madingley Hall, Cambridge, to Helpston, where they were to pay homage to the poet John Clare. It had been arranged that I should meet them in Peterborough Museum to give a brief, impromptu talk about Clare before they reached his village. This chance meeting led to my being invited to Roger's course the following year, where I was able to give a more formal lecture on the Helpston poet. Since then a friendship has been established which helps to explain why I was now out for a walk on that unspoilt margin that separates one country from another. (Perhaps I should also say that our visit to Bettws-y-Crwyn, and the affair with the llama, was only part of a longer holiday we were enjoying in Herefordshire.)

Why is it, I wonder, that one feels instinctively that there are certain times of the year when we must be in a certain place and nowhere else? This seems unerringly true for me. Take Christmas, for instance. Only two of my many Christmases have been spent away from home – and where better to be on such occasions than in the snow-stilled city of old Salzburg! But, if I am to feel really at home, really at ease, secure and comfortable, then it has to be in the place where for more than sixty years Christmas has been celebrated quietly with a few friends and family.

Easter, though, is a different matter. For some strange and adventurous reason, I always want to be somewhere else, away from home and the familiar landscape. It's as if this season is the gateway to a new year of experience and discovery. The long dark months are over; it is time to be up and about.

It is not that I like Easter necessarily less than Christmas; I still protect all those memories of childhood Easters with their chocolate eggs, rabbits, flowers in the house, and usually a new pair of shoes to wear for Sunday School. Yet, as I see it, it was always such a brief festival, and one was never quite sure when it was going to be – unlike Christmas, it changed from year to year. (I still find this very confusing. Why fix one important Christian festival and not the other, when, clearly, they are both connected?) I did not know then that Easter Day was governed by the first Sunday after the Paschal full moon, which occurs on the day of the vernal equinox or any of the next twenty-eight days. It was just a weekend that was different and, whether one was a believer or not, gave us the first real opportunity of an escape from the long shadows of winter.

For the past few years my wife and I have gone for the warmer climates of Spain, Majorca or Greece, where the bizarre religious processions have been more like carnivals, and the Holy Communion services have been accompanied by fire-crackers as well as incense. But this year we chose to settle for a quieter retreat in England, away from crowded airports and luggage trolleys. It is a little place in the Kyre Valley of Herefordshire called, appropriately, Stoke Bliss – and, for obvious reasons, I do not intend to give you more information than that.

What we did not know when we booked the cottage – which has been most imaginatively created out of a ruined cider-press and hop-kiln – was that we were to be blessed with Mediterranean weather. It felt as if April had leap-frogged over May and June right into July, with temperatures in the seventies and days of bright, translucent skies.

We had already had a few previous holidays there, but these had been in summer, or autumn. Now we wanted to see what it would be like in spring. We were certainly not to be disappointed. There was a quality of unpolluted light over the undulating countryside that made us believe we had settled somewhere near the Aegean Sea. The lane to the cottage was bordered with creamy clusters of primroses, gem-like violets and brassy daffodils.

This is sheep country, and most of the fields were already full of fat ewes and their new-born lambs. These were the scenes we were to have from each of the cottage windows for the two weeks of our stay: sheep, wild flowers, awakening hills, and expansive skies that provided a showcase for the sun.

One of the advantages we look forward to in Stoke Bliss (which is almost six miles from the nearest small town), is the joy of seeing again a really dark sky, unsullied by the contamination of artificial light from towns that have forgotten the true meaning of night. Here the immense sweep of stars is always impressive, but our first night was to give us even greater excitement. As well as all the usual sparkling constellations we had the best sighting we were likely to get of the Hale-Bopp comet. We had been disappointed at home because the skies had been too cloudy, but now, at Stoke Bliss, conditions were perfect. Here, among the favourite and familiar lights of heaven, was a stranger, a traveller through Time, and it shone with awesome majesty – proud and imperious, its long tail trailing across the sky like a regal, jewel-studded train. I soon realized that if one did not look directly at the comet itself but slightly off-focus from it – from the corner of the eye almost – the tail was even more magnificent and multicoloured. We were reluctant to take ourselves back indoors but, as we were tired after our journey and the clocks were being put forward one hour, we decided enough was enough. And, of course, tomorrow was Easter Sunday – not a day for a lie-in. So we left the comet to make its own way into the unknown for a few more thousand years.

We woke in the morning to the sound of a cockerel crowing triumphantly. The sun was already up, making the frost on the grass sparkle. After breakfast it was even warm enough for us to sit outside. Slowly the sheep, which had earlier looked like grey boulders half-buried in the grass, unthawed and gathered their young lambs around them. It was peaceful but not silent for, apart from the stuttering lambs, there was the sound of a man ploughing three fields away; the drone of his tractor buzzed like a persistent bee at the sky's window. Yet there was a stillness, like the stillness of clouds waiting for a wind to push them along. I wouldn't have minded then hearing the distant clangour of church bells to remind me that it was Easter Sunday. But there were no bells. The day stood poised in a world and time of its own making. I, for one, was not sorry that we had chosen to stay away from crowded airports and that anxious quest for the sun. This year the sun had come to us.

Several of my friends in the Fens are surprised that I can be so enthusiastic about another landscape, especially one that is so different. But that, surely, is one of the answers. Opposites often fulfil a need. After too much wine a glass of water can be sweetly refreshing. If I want to spend a few weeks living above sea-level for a change, then this is the part of England where I like to be, in a gentle terrain of low hills, rich green fields, sinuous rivers, yet with still enough space and sky to enjoy distance and light.

The valley of Kyre has a long history. The fields between our rented cottage and the brook are, for the time being, protected from excavation or development because they still retain rare plants, herbs and the star-shaped silver thistles left behind by the last Ice Age. But the area has other attractions for me besides those provided by nature. It is, after all, the heart of English music, of the Three Choirs Festivals, of Elgar, Vaughan Williams, Ivor Gurney and Gerald Finzi. Then there are the literary associations – Shakespeare, A.E. Housman, Francis Kilvert and Thomas Traherne.

One of the most vivid memories of our stay here a year ago was the day we went to Credenhill, the village where Traherne was the parish priest and wrote many of his poems: poems which were to remain unknown and lost for more than two hundred years. Even when they were discovered in 1896 on a London bookstall, they were thought to be by Henry Vaughan. It took the scholarship of Bertram Dobell to restore their true identity and to reveal to the world what a pure vision Traherne had, in both his poetry and his prose.

This gentlest of English poets was born in Herefordshire in 1637, the son of a shoemaker who died whilst Thomas was still a boy. He was then brought up by his uncle, who was twice Mayor of Hereford and who paid for his nephew to go to Brasenose College, Oxford, when he was sixteen years old. Three years later he took his BA, and in 1660 was ordained deacon and priest. A year later he accepted the living at Credenhill. After eight happy and creative years in his native Herefordshire he was appointed chaplain to Sir Orlando Bridgeman and moved to Teddington, where he died in 1674 at the age of 37.

The church and the village are now separated by a very busy road. We made our way up the narrow lane half-expecting the church door to be locked, as it would have been had we gone on any other morning of the week except Sunday. We'd had the good fortune to go on the one weekday when there was a morning Communion service. As we stepped inside it was as if we had crossed three centuries. The priest stood at the altar, and one lady knelt in the chancel alone. In the candle-lit stillness it could have been Traherne himself offering up the Host for a blessing. We stood in the shadows of the nave and waited until the service came to an end, knowing that we, too, had shared in a special moment. Afterwards, when we walked round the churchyard, we were surprised to find about thirty graves with simple wooden crosses, on each of which was a Polish surname. We found out later that these were of Polish airmen who had died in exile, survivors of a war that was for them the night in which their own faith was betrayed. Many had survived the war but had spent their last years in this quiet corner of England, where their bones were finally laid to rest.

Another Herefordshire church with literary associations is the small twelfth-century church at Brinsop. In 1824 the manor house was leased to Thomas Hutchinson, who was the brother of William Wordsworth's wife, Mary. The Wordsworths, including William's sister Dorothy, were frequent visitors to Brinsop and worshipped in this little church, where there are now stained-glass windows to their memory. Robert Southey was also a visitor; so, too, was Francis Kilvert, who recorded in his diary on 13 March 1879 that he took the train to Credenhill, walked up to the church where Traherne had preached, then under the wood to Brinsop:

> Little Brinsop Church lay peacefully below among the meadows of the Brinsop Vale. Had lunch at Brinsop Vicarage. . . . In the afternoon I walked with Mr Fowle to the church. . . . A fine sunset gleam lit up the grand old manor house. . . . On the lawn grew the cedar planted by William Wordsworth. . . . Back to Brinsop Vicarage to tea and then I was driven to Credenhill Station to catch the 8.10 train.

Put all these interests together and it is not surprising that I find the county and its surrounding countryside so appealing.

And this year came the encounter with the llama who took a fancy to me. How lucky can you be! It was not an affection I would wish to receive every Sunday afternoon, but I was flattered by that first experience. She was a graceful, noble, tender-hearted creature for whom I had a lot of admiration.

A week later we were back home in the Fens which, in our absence, had also blossomed in the exceptionally warm days of April. In fact the advanced spring was even more noticeable. At Stoke Bliss the daffodils were still a fresh, crimped yellow, and the chestnut trees had progressed only as far as their spiky, gummy buds. Those in Cambridgeshire were already in leaf and would soon be ready for their bloom of candles. The lime trees, too, welcomed our return with one of the loveliest greens of spring – pale, flake-like and shimmering in the morning sun. The cherry-blossom was out; so, too, was the lilac. It needed something special to compensate for the beauties we had left behind in another county.

So, with my urge to be somewhere different for Easter satisfied, it is time to settle down again to the old routine – not that my routine is one to grumble about. It is always good to come back home to normality, to pick up old habits and enjoy the common-place. I feel as much at one with Traherne in the Fens as I do with him in Herefordshire and am consoled when he writes:

> And what rule do you think I walked by? Truly a strange one, but the best in the whole world. I was guided by an implicit faith in God's goodness, and therefore led to the study of the most obvious and common things. . . . For nothing is more natural to infinite goodness than to make the best things most frequent, and only things worthless scarce. Then I began to enquire what things were most common: air, light, heaven and earth, water, the sun, trees, men and women, cities, temples, etc. These I found common and obvious to all. Rubies, pearls, diamonds, gold and silver, these I found scarce and to most denied.

Earlier in the same *Meditation* he had written:

> I was so resolute that I chose rather to live upon £10 a year, so that I might have all my time clearly to myself, than to keep many thousands per annum in an estate of life where my time would be devoured in care and labour.

I think you know me well enough by now to appreciate why the writings of Traherne and Henry David Thoreau appeal to me as much as they do. They put life, as I wish to see it, into perspective and made the simple, commonplace things essential to the contentment of the untroubled mind. Perhaps it was easier to achieve that state in the seventeenth and nineteenth centuries than it is now, but I still think it is an ideal worth pursuing. How else are we going to keep sane?

P.S. I have just picked up a local newspaper and, would you believe it, there is a photograph of a baby llama and its mother who were a recent attraction at some event at Peckover House, Wisbech. So they *are* here!

❧ 9 ❧

Having Seen it for Ourselves

I seem to make a habit of letting myself in for all kinds of occupa-
tions which originally, and innocently, I saw as straightforward
engagements. The most recent of these was as a voluntary tour-
guide. No, not through the South of France or the Dolomites, not
even in Scotland or the West Country, but (surprise, surprise!)
through the Fens.

It was, I graciously concede, a most delightful and satisfying
experience, and I could not have had a better, more obedient party
of tourists to take round. It is only fair to explain that I had met
most of them before, because they are members of the
Peterborough and District Branch of the Parkinson's Disease
Society, for whom I annually give an evening's entertainment in the
autumn. It was as a result of my visit last September that I received
a request to take a coach-party on a tour of the Fens the following
spring.

The only other time I have agreed to do such a thing was many
years ago when the weather was completely the opposite of the
conditions I had prayed for. October can be very beautiful, after all,
but that year it was not. It was grey, damp and depressing on the
chosen day – a day so ashamed of itself that it seemed to hurry
towards its own demise. Where were those great open spaces, those
far distant horizons, that sparkling light and vibrant landscape with
which I had seduced my audience only two months before? Gone!
Wrapped in the shrouds of an autumn which I had trusted would be
kinder, but wasn't. I vowed I would never do it again. Although the
people on that excursion were good-humoured and understanding,
I knew that the day had not come up to expectations.

One takes an enormous risk when agreeing to show off a landscape, especially that of the Fens. When it is so intimately known

throughout every season of the year, you want it to be at its best when shown to others. But, as the secretary of the Parkinson's Disease Society pleaded, there was a much better chance of the conditions being more favourable in April than October. So I gave in and approached the day with a mixture of hope and trepidation.

I need not have worried, for when it arrived we found ourselves in the middle of a mini-heatwave, with temperatures more suitable for July or Majorca. Personally I prefer there to be a few ranges of cumulus in our skies, because they help to give perspective to the space, but I was not about to grumble – even though some of the photographers I know would have (for them an infinite royal-blue backdrop is just not what they want for a dramatic, moody picture.) I was simply grateful that we had been granted an April evening of such warmth and pure light that we could all forget about it being the eve of a General Election – anything for a few hours away from those television commentators gloating over possible disasters, landslides and political burials before even a vote had been cast.

Our departure was scheduled for four o'clock, and everyone was on time. I was pleased to learn that for many of my group this would be their first real view of the Fens. There were people of all ages and backgrounds, some from London, others from Cornwall, some from Derbyshire and those from the north-east. For various reasons they had come to live in the area and now, because of their illness, had little chance of exploring the countryside for themselves. Even those who were local had not ventured into the obscure corners where I was planning to take them. My only concern was that our driver would not be able to get his posh coach down some of the narrow Fenland droves or round those awkward bends suitable only for tractors. But when he told me that he had just returned from a tour of the Lake District, was used to driving through the Devon lanes, and had taken many trips to the Continent, I relaxed. He was great.

Soon we were untangling ourselves from the noisy city streets and making our way to Holme Fen. Before turning off the main road to slip through the old part of the village of Yaxley, I pointed out that a few hundred yards to our right, near the A1, had once been the Norman Cross Prison Camp, built in 1796 at a cost of £35,000. (You may remember from my second letter that this was the Depot to which the young Harry Smith was posted when he joined the Yeoman Cavalry in 1804). Apart from the Governor's House, the camp was constructed entirely of timber and had employed five hundred carpenters. During the prison's twenty-year history an estimated seven thousand men were held there. Until other camps were built the one at Norman Cross sometimes became so over-crowded that during the summer months many of the prisoners were made to sleep in the open compounds, rather than risk suffocation in the hot, crowded cells. In winter they had no choice and slept in three-tiered hammocks, with no heating and very little daylight. Food was scarce, and the camp was to suffer several serious epidemics. Almost two thousand prisoners were to die at Norman Cross, their bodies buried in a field next to the now congested A1 road that throbs with the noise of lorries from France, Germany, Italy and Scandinavia, as well as England.

Some of the prisoners tried to escape, but few succeeded in getting out of what was a well-guarded fortress. The few who did were later picked up on their way to one of the east-coast ports – Wisbech, King's Lynn, or Boston. In 1807 prisoners in one section of the camp decided to storm the main gates, but British soldiers with fixed bayonets were waiting for them on the other side, and more than sixty of the Frenchmen were seriously wounded and put into solitary confinement.

It was hardly the most cheerful of stories with which to commence an introduction to the beauties of the Fens, but one of my passengers was pleased that I had mentioned it because he was interested in the Governor's House, which, he said, reminded him of the sea-captains' houses he knew in Cornwall. One of the ladies in the party then told me how grateful she was to learn that the commanding officer at Norman Cross had been the father of the writer George Borrow, who frequently stayed there.

Before changing the subject I felt I also had to say something about the remarkable craftsmanship which many of those prisoners developed during their years of captivity, particularly in the art of bone-carving and straw-marquetry. Because much of their work has been preserved in our local museums, especially at Peterborough, we can appreciate the exquisite work they created out of very basic materials and crude implements. The bones were saved from what meat the men were allowed – or collected from the local girls, who were sometimes permitted to visit the prison with food parcels or to return laundry – and then carved into models of ships, carriages, houses and jewellery. The prisoners' unique straw-plaiting was equally beautiful, and I even found some of it at the Spalding Gentlemen's Society museum.

When the Napoleonic Wars were eventually over not all the prisoners returned to France. Quite a few had fallen in love with local girls and were granted the right to stay here and marry. About twenty years ago I was talking to an elderly lady in Yaxley who told me that her great-grandfather had been a prisoner at Norman Cross. She made it sound like yesterday.

But let me get back to our evening journey through the more peaceful Fens and a few other pages of their history. Our first stop was to see the Holme Fen Post which has been recording the alarming shrinkage of the Fens since Whittlesea Mere was drained in 1851. I should really say *Posts*, for, as I will explain in a moment, there are now two. Before getting to them we had to pause for a few moments at the railway crossing to allow an elegant express train to go by like a flash of lightning in its new GNER livery, introduced with privatization. The railway track and superstructure for the electricity cables of this line have to be carefully maintained and reinforced against the continual shrinking of the land over which it passes. Consequently it is now several feet higher than the surrounding countryside, providing the travellers (those who are not on their mobile phones or working a computer) with an excellent view of the Fens.

The purpose of taking these people to see the posts was to demonstrate just how disconcerting the problem of soil-shrinkage has been during the last 140 years. The decision to drain the Mere caused much controversy at the time, for it was believed that if the water were taken from it, the land, being mostly peat, would rapidly shrink when exposed to the air and wind. To prove the point a 12-ft cast-iron post, taken from the dismantling of the Great Exhibition Hall in London in 1851, was driven like a nail into the ground until it disappeared. A hundred years later that post was completely revealed again and had to be held up by steel guy-ropes. A new post was then erected next to it to continue measuring the rate of soil erosion. If, as you stand there today, all that soil could be restored, you would be buried more than twenty feet below what had once been ground level. Or, to put it another way, you are now standing at eight feet below sea-level, at the lowest point in England. It's a sobering thought.

We stopped a little further along the single-track road to look over the farmland that was once Whittlesea Mere, a stretch of water that could be compared with Hickling Broad or Derwent Water, varying in size depending on the season. In winter it covered more

Holme Fen measuring post

than 3,000 acres but in summer-time could be as small as 1,800 acres. In the seventeenth and eighteenth centuries it was very popular as a sporting venue, especially for extravagant regattas, or water picnics as they were more often called then. On public holidays large crowds gathered at the Mere for a day's outing and to see the gentry in their decorated yachts and barges. There were side shows, craft stalls and various tradesmen selling their wares – hot pies, sausages, muffins, ales, trinkets and domestic tools, similar to what we would expect to find these days at an agricultural show or gymkhana. There was even a bandstand for groups of musicians to entertain the visitors. From the old prints I have seen of these occasions Whittlesea Mere must have offered one of the most attractive sights in the Fens.

I will not, if you don't mind, give you an itemized account of the rest of our trip. I will simply say that it included Ramsey, Chatteris, Christchurch, Upwell and Wisbech, before we reached our supper destination at the Woodman's Cottage, Gorefield. I had chosen this friendly Fenland pub because I knew that some of the men, and indeed a few of the ladies, would not be able to resist some of the very tempting desserts for which this hostelry is famous. You can imagine that, after three hours of talking about Hereward the Wake, Oliver Cromwell, Cornelius Vermuyden, Thomas Clarkson and Dorothy L. Sayers, my most immediate need was a cool pint of draught beer, one brewed in the neighbouring county of Suffolk.

Throughout our journey we had been lucky to have a view of the Fens at their golden best. This time the light was crystal clear, the sky limitless, the horizons truly far away, the water in the dykes and rivers mirror-bright in its stillness. We were never more than a few yards from water – Bevill's Leam, Forty Foot, Sixteen Foot, the old River Nene and a whole network of drains that lift the water from below sea-level into the main rivers that take it the rest of the way to the outfalls in the Wash. You can imagine what a Dutch scene this would have presented before the age of steam, when hundreds of windmills were needed to do the job of pumping. What we had seen instead were a dozen or more nesting swans curled white and silent as large meringues, and heard briefly the now almost rare skylark. This wonderful bird has been one of the saddest losses in the Fens during my lifetime. When I was a boy it was not uncommon to hear twenty or thirty displaying their coloratura skills high above the fields at the end of our street, but I was reading only the other day that there has been a sixty-per-cent decline in the number of skylarks during the last twenty-five years alone. What the fatality rate must be for the past fifty years hardly bears thinking about. If it is depressing to be told that in another thirty years' time children may not see any stars, it is equally tragic that before then they will probably not hear several of the songbirds we still take for granted. Blackbirds and thrushes have suffered even more than larks, as have bullfinches, linnets and doves. The problem, and the responsibility, belongs to more than one generation. (I did not intend to put on my Jeremiah cloak as soon as this, but the facts cannot be swept under the carpet, not even one as large as the Fens.)

When our supper was over we set off in that alluring light of a spring evening. The brash yellow of the rape crops was now a more mature, unpolished gold. Mist was rising from the dykes, and there was that lovely feeling of mystery that only a fenland twilight can create. We passed Parson Drove, Throckenholt, Gedney Hill, Whaplode Drove on our way to Crowland. There the ruins of the abbey were magically floodlit, giving the impression that the broken arches were carved out of alabaster. It was the perfect benediction on an excursion I would not have missed for all the world. My joy was complete when several of the group said what a wonderful experience it had been for them, to see the Fens as they had never seen them before, to have learnt a little of the complicated history of the area where they had come to live. As one lady put it, 'having seen it for ourselves we can now understand why the place means so much to you.'

After leaving this letter unfinished last night I return to it this morning knowing that, for the record, I have to put on my Jeremiah cloak again, if only to remind us all that this landscape which I praise so much is one we should not glibly ignore. Not only have we been losing the Fens through the natural erosion of the soil, there is also the serious threat of what would happen if global warming became a reality, as we are assured it will.

A report in *The Times*, (July 1996) stated that, if global warming continues, then the earth's temperature by the year 2030 will rise by 1.6°C, putting 150,000 acres of fenland back under water, particularly in Lincolnshire and Norfolk, with their close proximity to the sea. The Cambridgeshire Fens would not be spared either, because it would virtually become impossible to get the upland waters out into the Wash. With much of our land already below sea-level it is obvious what would happen if the oceans were expanded by the melting of extra ice from the Poles. Speculation, you might say? Possibly. Not all surveys turn out to be accurate, but the warning is there, and it would be foolish to be complacent. And, as someone pointed out to me on our trip, if a large expanse of the Fens went back to being wetland this could be both an advantage and an attraction. By reverting to their original state the Fens would again become a natural habitat for wildfowl and other threatened species, such as frogs, newts, snakes, otters, butterflies and flowers, as well as birds.

However, even if global warming does not happen within the thirty years forecast, there is still another threat: urban sprawl. A survey carried out for the Department of the Environment in 1996 showed that 21.3 per cent of rural Cambridgeshire could disappear by the year 2016 if present trends in development went unchecked. This would mean that more than 14,000 acres of farmland would be lost to make way for between 130,000 and 140,000 new houses. You can imagine what demands this would make on our public services, and how many extra cars would accelerate on to our already full roads.

It seems to me that we are losing more than the 10,000 miles of hedgerows that disappear in this country every year, more than the 20,000 acres of farmland, more even than the wild-life that goes with those losses. We are losing ourselves – and the tragedy is that we have only ourselves to blame. I agree that enthusiasm for a landscape has to be tempered with the hard realities of survival. But what do we mean by survival?

The kind of excursion that was taken by the Parkinson's Disease Society may itself be history before long, and we shall all be grateful that we saw the Fens for ourselves on such a day as the one given to us in April 1997. Now, after all those sombre thoughts, I feel a bit like the Welshman at his friend's funeral who, on hearing that Wales had been beaten by England at Cardiff Arms Park said, 'It cast a gloom over the entire proceedings.' Maybe I shall be out of mourning by the time I write to you again.

৩ 10 ৩

The World's Debt to Wisbech

If I were to ask you what Nova Scotia, Sierra Leone and Wisbech had in common, you could be forgiven for thinking that I was posing one of those humiliating conundrums that we were asked in primary school aeons ago.

I could make the riddle even more puzzling if I then asked what Canterbury, Rome and Wisbech had in common. I could even complicate matters by asking if you knew of the connection between the Lake District, America, Westminster Abbey and Wisbech.

Whatever permutation I chose to tease you, it would, I'm sure, not take you long to work out that the key to solving this mystery was Wisbech. And, although I do not propose to give you a potted history of the town, I should remind you that eight hundred years ago it was an important port on the east coast, that its sea trade was largely responsible for its wealth, and that the sea then lapped at its parish boundary. Now the sea is a dozen miles away, and the port's trade has been surrendered to King's Lynn. What also helped in this transfer of power was the straightening out of the Great Ouse, which made Lynn the point at which the river met The Wash. This, and the changing coastline, meant that Wisbech came to rely more and more on farming, fruit-growing and banking.

Of all Fenland towns it must surely be the place that has produced the greatest number of men and women who have served the needs of mankind, thereby achieving fame where it was not sought. One thinks especially of the Clarkson brothers, Thomas and John, who were two of the most active pioneers in the abolition of the slave trade; of Octavia Hill, a co-founder of the National Trust and founder of the Octavia Hill Housing Trust in London; and of the Peckover family, the Quaker bankers who were influential benefactors with a particular concern for the provision of education for all.

I shall return to these illustrious citizens later, but there are other names which should be added to the town's honours board, such as Thomas Herring, who became Archbishop of Canterbury in 1747; Nicholas Breakspeare, who, though not Fen-born, lived for many years at nearby Tydd St Giles before being chosen to become Pope Adrian IV in 1154; and Samuel Smith, a pioneer photographer in the nineteenth century, who saw the camera as an important recorder of history. There was also William Godwin, the philosopher and novelist, who spent his childhood in Wisbech; Dr Richard Middleton Massey, the eminent physician who lived in the town for twenty-two years, and George Guest, the well-known organist and hymn-writer who was resident from 1789 to 1831. The list is by no means exhausted, but if I continued to add to it this letter would end up as a *Who's Who* of Wisbech, and there would be no space for me to enlarge on any of their achievements, though I promise to return to some.

So where do I stop, or where do I start? And what sparked off this latest interest in the celebrities of a town I have written about often enough before? After all, you can't live in the Fen country all your life without being aware of what has been happening in one of its most independent and historical places. But my enthusiasm for it has grown over the years because I have been fortunate in having several good friends there, including Dr Peter Cave and his wife Margaret, who two years ago was the town mayor and in charge of the 150th Anniversary Appeal to get Thomas Clarkson commemorated in Westminster Abbey. Although I have touched on the achievements of Thomas Clarkson, Octavia Hill, and the Peckover family in my previous books, it was not until I was talking to Peter earlier this year that I realized that I had not done them justice. I felt, as I had about Sir Harry Smith, that to know the bare bones was not enough. I needed to inform myself more about the lives, deeds and triumphs that had earned these figures a worthy place in our history. So I invited myself over to Wisbech to gather, glean and grab as much information as I could from Peter's and Margaret's files. Thank goodness both of them are great hoarders of newspaper-cuttings, reports, documents and journals which, as they say, 'might come in handy one of these days'. Because they have both been members of the Wisbech Society for many years their local knowledge is vast.

As I approached the town, with the elegant houses of North Brink on my left, I was greeted by a fierce and sudden hailstorm. This had one advantage, because the dark sky provided an admirable backdrop to the tall Thomas Clarkson memorial, one of the last works of Sir George Gilbert Scott. The town has made sure that no one forgets its famous sons and daughters by perpetuating their names in a number of ways. The Caves, appropriately, live in Clarkson Avenue, and the *Clarkson Arms* public house is opposite the entrance to their road. There are others, but I won't list them all now.

Our discussions began over an excellent working lunch, and by the time that was over I already began to feel that I was about to embark on a three-volume History of Wisbech, rather than one or two short letters. So many names had been mentioned, so many important episodes listed. Bound volumes of The Wisbech Society's Annual Reports were produced, together with copies of its other publications about the town's achievements, and there were names and addresses of other people I should contact. When I left the house my arms were laden with packages, books, files and memorabilia. I felt as if I had robbed a bank, and couldn't wait to examine the loot.

You probably know what risks there are in reading old newspapers. There is always another story on the opposite page that intrigues as much as the one you are supposed to be reading, and you can't resist it. The one that caught my eye was about Jane Stuart, the illegitimate daughter of James II. What was she doing in Wisbech? And how did she come to be interred in the Burial Ground of the Friends' Meeting House on North Brink? It is a sad and extraordinary story and there are some historians who doubt whether it is all true. But I am going to give you the version I read, because it is the one I want to believe.

Jane was brought to this country when she was six years old, the daughter of a French girl who had been a maid-of-honour to the mother of James, who was then Duke of York and in exile with his family. She became one of James's mistresses and eventually bore him a daughter whom he openly acknowledged as his child. Jane's parentage was no secret even when the family returned to England. Although she was brought up in the Catholic faith she transferred her sympathies to the Quakers when she fell in love with the man she wanted to marry. The marriage was arranged, not without opposition and acrimony, but on their way to the ceremony the coach in which the bride and bridegroom were travelling was mysteriously overturned, and the young man was killed. Jane went back to her rooms to mourn alone until the abdication of her father in 1688. Then, at the age of thirty-four, she left London in disguise and began her long trek to Wisbech. Why Wisbech, you may ask? I don't know. Maybe she had already established Quaker contacts there, but the newspaper report said that she arrived penniless and friendless. A few days later she watched some of the local farm labourers who had gathered at the bridge hoping to be hired out for work, and decided to join them. When one of the farmers asked her if she could reap she replied, 'I do not know until I have tried.' He liked her reply and offered to teach her. She soon became so skilled at the task that her fellow-workers, still not knowing who she was, called her Queen of Reapers.

Jane Stuart decided that Wisbech was the place where she could spend her days contentedly in obscurity and found a simple home for herself in the cellar of a house in the old Market Place. Here she taught herself to spin and weave, and was soon able to set up stall on the weekly markets to sell her work. Meanwhile her two half-sisters, Mary II and Anne, successively occupied the dubious throne of England, little knowing that Jane was living the life of a peasant in the Fens.

How many people knew of her secret it is difficult to tell. A few of her closest Quaker friends in Wisbech must have known but, true to their faith, kept it to themselves. She found sufficient solace in Wisbech to remain there until she was eighty-eight years old, dying on 12 July 1742. She was laid to rest in the Friends' own Burial Ground behind the Quaker Meeting House, her grave bordered still to this day by a trim box hedge, as if to protect both the memory and the mystery of this enigmatic lady.

But, I can now hear you saying, when am I going to start telling you about Thomas and John Clarkson? I agree that, quite unintentionally, I have kept you in suspense far too long. But, having written this much, I now find there is little time left to give you an adequate account of either man in one letter. Nevertheless, I will endeavour to tell you briefly something about John, Thomas's younger brother by four years, if only to show you how Nova Scotia, Sierra Leone, and Wisbech came to be so interwoven.

John Clarkson was born on 4 April 1764. His father, the Reverend John Clarkson, was the headmaster of the old Grammar School in the town but died before his youngest son had reached his second birthday. When John was only thirteen years old it was decided that he should go into the Navy; his older brother Thomas was destined, so it was thought at the time, for a brilliant career in the church.

The English Navy in the eighteenth century would have been a shocking baptism into adulthood for such a gentle, humorous, liberal-minded boy. Most ship's crew were made up of men press-ganged into service and flogged into submission. John was to see active service in four major sea battles before winning his first commission as a lieutenant. His career began at the same time as the American Revolution but, by the time that war was over, the Navy's need of officers had been reduced so rapidly that there was little chance of further promotion for a young officer. Even worse was the prospect of being without a ship.

It would have been uncharacteristic of the Clarkson family for the youngest son to remain idle and at home for long, and it was no surprise when John asked to become involved in his brother's one-man campaign to abolish the slave trade which was then flourishing in England. So let me put you in the picture about him as well.

Thomas Clarkson was born on 28 March 1760 and was educated at St Paul's, London, and St John's College, Cambridge, where his tutors were already predicting that he would one day become at least a bishop. He had already won the Latin Essay Competition in 1785 when the Vice-Chancellor of the college set the bachelors a new contest on the question 'Is it lawful to make slaves of others against their will?' Although Thomas knew very little about the slave trade, he decided to enter. Slavery was then still acceptable to most people in this country, and a great deal of our commerce depended on it. Only the Quakers and that courageous man Granville Sharp were striving to get the evil system abolished. Even the scandal of the captain of the slave ship *Zong*, who threw his cargo of 132 sick slaves overboard and then tried to collect insurance compensation, failed to stir the nation's conscience into protest or action. The law, Parliament and commerce, seemed united in making sure that slavery should continue as a rightful and necessary condition of blacks in a white society. Africans were not people, they were possessions.

Thomas Clarkson's research into slavery filled him with horror and disgust. He now believed he had discovered his purpose in life: not to become a scholar or a bishop, but to campaign vigorously throughout the land to abolish this inhumane practice. At the time

Britain was the greatest slave-trader in the world, shipping thousands of slaves each year into the West Indies and then America.

Clarkson's essay not only won the contest but was warmly received by the Quakers, who agreed to publish an extended version of it in 1786. To everyone's surprise it became a bestseller. And so his life's work began, touring the countryside, mostly on horseback, lecturing in the cities, raising money, gathering statistics, interviewing seamen who had worked on the slave ships, and publishing drawings of the atrocious conditions in which the slaves were being transported. He visited those ports where the trade was most thriving – London, Chatham, Liverpool, Manchester and Bristol. He was abused, physically assaulted and denied access to the docks, yet he still managed to collect evidence from 20,000 sailors who had crewed the ships and learned from them of the relentless brutality they had witnessed. He was tireless. The poet Coleridge was to call him 'a moral steam-engine' and a 'giant with one idea'.

It is not surprising that his zeal and vision were to have such a decisive influence on his brother John who, having no job, was equally keen to take up the cause. John's great asset was his maritime knowledge and experience at sea. He had sailed to Spain, Africa and America, and knew people in important places who might be persuaded to listen. His first task was to help the black slaves who had sided with Britain during the American Revolution. They had been granted asylum in Nova Scotia but, once there, were often treated as badly as before. Many of them now wanted to return to Africa and asked the English abolitionists to help. John Clarkson volunteered to organize a rescue mission and to transport them back home, to the colony that was to become known as Freetown, Sierra Leone. By the time the exodus was ready he had assembled a fleet of fifteen ships under his command. Inspired by Granville Sharp he even wanted to settle with the Africans in their new country, to prove that colour need not be a barrier to people of different cultures living together. Little did he realize that he would become the first Governor of the Sierra Leone Company and win the affection of most of those people he had helped to save.

There were many who wished he had stayed with them for the rest of his life, but the Sierra Leone Trading Company decided that it was time for a change, and John returned home to England to help with the founding of the Society for Promotion of Permanent and Universal Peace – what a forward-looking man he was. To help fund his causes he also entered banking and became a successful lime-manufacturer. In addition to all these activities he married and became the father of ten children, six of whom predeceased him.

Despite all this he remains a mostly unsung hero in the shadow of his more famous brother. If you would like to know more about him I urge you to read Ellen Gibson Wilson's biography *John Clarkson and the African Adventure* (Macmillan, 1980). It is an inspiring testimony to what one individual can achieve when self is put second to the needs of others. John Clarkson, too, deserves his monument.

Mrs Wilson has also written an excellent biography of Thomas Clarkson, but I shall have to tell you more about that another time.

ᥱᓅ 11 ᡠᥱ

Such a Grand Piece of Clay

You will have gathered from my last letter that there is so much to tell you about the Clarkson brothers that one is in danger of tripping over one's own enthusiasm. So I will try to make this episode a little more orderly.

On 26 September 1996 a memorial stone was unveiled in Westminster Abbey to honour the name of Thomas Clarkson. It is close to the more elaborate monument erected to the memory of William Wilberforce who, until recently, had received virtually all the credit for the abolition of the slave trade. The unveiling of the Clarkson stone also marked the 150th anniversary of his death.

Once again I am indebted to Peter and Margaret Cave for their willingness to let me pluck from their files the facts that help to give substance to my enthusiasm. They, together with a select committee of dedicated Clarksonians, worked diligently to raise the money needed for a memorial in the Abbey, and to get their application accepted – which is no mere formality, as I know from when the John Clare Society wished to get the poet's name perpetuated in Poets' Corner.

In addition to the unveiling of the Clarkson memorial, which followed Evensong, the anniversary celebrations included exhibitions, drama productions, lectures and concerts, bringing together many people who shared his concern for all people who were victims of oppression.

Clarkson was a colossus, a man with such a presence that, even when he was close to death, anyone in his company responded with awe. His wife said of him: 'He was such a grand piece of clay that the persons employed went out of the room backwards, as if in the presence of a monarch.'

Such a description might mistakenly portray him as a proud,

autocratic man, rather than one of humility and great strength of character. The fact that at the age of twenty-five he chose to forfeit a promising career in order to devote his whole life to the slaves' cause, proves he was a man of compassion, conviction and service. By the time that slavery was abolished forty-two years later he had been responsible for helping to liberate 800,000 slaves throughout the British Empire and making sure that millions followed.

So why, you are probably asking, are we only just beginning to learn of this man's tremendous role in the campaign? It is a long and complicated story. Although Clarkson himself – a Quaker in spirit if not in admission – did not want any praise or aggrandizement, he was in effect deliberately written out of history by the Wilberforce family. In 1838, when Thomas Clarkson was seventy-eight and almost blind, William Wilberforce's sons (one a bishop and the other an archbishop) published a biography of their father in which they carefully minimized Clarkson's part in the abolition of the slave trade so that their father should get all the glory, as he did. By public demand and subscription Wilberforce was soon given his place in Westminster Abbey, and consequently his place in history. The deception was handed on to posterity, and only recently have scholars been able to put the record straight.

Later generations of the Wilberforce family admitted that it was wrong to condemn Thomas Clarkson to the shadows, and there has been a reconciliation, with both families coming together at the unveiling of the Clarkson memorial plaque. But it takes a long time for misjudgements in history to be corrected, in Clarkson's case 150 years. As I see it, both men should now share equal recognition, because neither would have succeeded without the other. During their lifetime they worked amicably towards the same end. Clarkson needed someone to present his case before Parliament; Wilberforce, a genuine opponent of slavery, wanted someone to present him with the facts. Clarkson was not a committee man. He was a researcher and campaigner. He went out single-handed to collect evidence and to stir the nation's conscience.

The voluminous and damning reports he sent to Wilberforce revealed an appalling industry in human life, for which Britain was largely responsible. But not even the eloquence of the persuasive Wilberforce could move Parliament into action to begin with –

there were too many vested interests. On 12 May 1789 he spoke to the House for three and a half hours, only to have the bill postponed until a further inquiry had been carried out.

Meanwhile, Clarkson was gathering more and more evidence. He toured all the main ports and dockyards, boarded 317 ships to interview their crews and to inspect the accommodation. He wrote hundreds of pamphlets and gave countless lectures, often to hostile audiences.

As part of his campaign he arranged with the Wedgwood family to produce a china cameo in black and white, showing a slave kneeling in chains, pleading with his master – indeed, with the whole of mankind. The question it asked was simple and searching: 'Am I not a man and a brother?' It was produced in thousands, and Clarkson personally gave away many hundreds. Women, who were not allowed to sign any of the anti-slavery petitions (still being partly in chains themselves), had it set into brooches, bracelets and hat-pins as a positive way of showing their support.

Clarkson's concern for the slaves, who were still seen merely as the chattels and soulless possessions of their masters, persisted to the end of his life. Yet it is worth reminding ourselves that he was a man of many other interests. He loved literature, especially poetry, which he occasionally wrote; he also had a passion for history, music and philosophy. In addition to that, he was a farmer and the author of twenty-four books as well as innumerable pamphlets, and he was the first non-Quaker to write a full history of the Society of Friends. All these talents simply emphasize the scale of his dedication to the abolition of the slave-trade.

Sympathies are all very well, but unless you know how to apply them to the practical needs of reform they remain fairly passive. Clarkson's unique approach was the use of something we are beginning to look upon as an infringement of our rights: unsolicited publicity. He was probably the first man to appreciate the power of advertising. Another of his effective publications was the drawing of a packed slave ship, showing the negroes stored side by side, like sardines. This was circulated to thousands of homes, framed and hung on the walls, rather like those illustrated biblical texts which were once so fashionable.

The message was at least getting through to the people if not Parliament. Poets also lent their support by writing verses about the plight of the slaves. William Cowper (1731-1800) who wrote 'God moves in a mysterious way His wonders to perform', declared:

I own I am shocked at the purchase of slaves,
And fear those who buy them and sell them are knaves;
What I hear of their hardships, their tortures and groans,
Is almost enough to draw pity from stones.

But many hearts were still harder than stones, and Cowper indulged
in a rare moment of sarcasm:

I pity them greatly, but I must be mum,
For how could we do without sugar and rum?
Especially sugar, so needful we see.
What! Give up our desserts, our coffee and tea!

Besides, if we do, the French, Dutch and Danes
Will heartily thank us no doubt for our pains. . .

It was not great poetry – propaganda poetry seldom is – but it
was all helping to persuade people to boycott trade with the West
Indies and bring an element of guilt to our back doors, as in these
lines from Cowper's *The Negro's Complaint*:

Men from England bought and sold me,
   Paid my price in paltry gold;
But, slave though they have enrolled me,
   Minds are never to be sold. . . . .

Skins may differ, but affection
   Dwells in white and black the same.

These were courageous statements to make at the time, but I
believe all acts of mercy, convictions of conscience and condemna-
tions of injustice need courage, as Thomas Clarkson discovered.
Reforms are not brought about overnight or painlessly. As Edmund
Burke was to say in his speech on conciliation with America on 22
March 1775: 'The march of the human mind is slow' and 'slavery
. . . is a weed that grows in every soil.' It is as old as Man himself.
The Old Testament gives a vivid account of how the Egyptians
treated the Hebrew slaves, and yet we still admire the pyramids
they built. Nor did slavery end with the success of Clarkson and
Wilberforce. It still exists in parts of the Third World today, as do
many forms of cruel child labour. We have to remind ourselves of
the subject that was set for the essay Clarkson was to write in 1785,

'Is it lawful to make slaves of others against their will?', to know that underprivileged people can always be exploited by others in the name of commerce, industry, progress.

There was still plenty of work for Thomas Clarkson and his growing number of supporters to do, because the opposition (known as the West Indian lobby) was very powerful, with share-holders ranging from Government officials to widows. Delaying tactics were seen as a potent weapon against the Abolitionists' demands for action. So the House of Commons inquiry continued for two years, and it was not until 18 April 1791 that Wilberforce was again able to put his bill before Parliament. The debate went on until the early hours of the morning and, when the vote came at 3.30 a.m., the bill was defeated by 163 votes to 88. There was clearly still a long way to go before all men were free or equal. The feared outcome of abolition was being compared by its opponents with the French Revolution, and Thomas Clarkson was seen as dangerous a man as Tom Paine, the author of *The Rights of Man*.

Many more years of struggle were needed before the slave-trade was abolished in 1807, and slavery itself finally banned in the British Empire in 1833. Wilberforce was not to enjoy the success of their efforts, though. During the latter years of the campaign he had been suffering a serious illness, and he died in July 1833. Clarkson lived for a further thirteen years and died in September 1846. The friendship and respect that the two men had shown each other over so many years was put in question by the publication in 1838 of Wilberforce's biography, written by his two sons who loaded the scales in their father's favour, leaving Clarkson in old age to ponder ruefully on being discarded and then labelled by them as 'a shabby old romantic'. This unkind description was a pathetic reference to the warm friendship that the Clarksons had enjoyed with the Wordsworths, Coleridges and Charles Lamb.

Again I am grateful to Ellen Gibson Wilson for her thorough research into the history of the abolition movement. Her scholarship is of great value to us all. Fortunately her biography of Thomas Clarkson (first published in 1989 by Macmillan) has just been reis-sued by William Sessions Ltd (1996) and should be on all our library shelves. It is a magnificent tribute to one man's determination to see justice done.

Before leaving the subject I must say something more about the unusual period of the Clarksons' lives when they lived for a time on the shores of Ullswater and found they had much in common with the Lakeland poets. Dorothy Wordsworth, that prodigious letter-writer and journal-keeper, considered Catherine Clarkson one of her greatest and most loved friends. The two families even contemplated sharing the same house, so close were they in their interests, affections and beliefs. Dorothy's journal gives repeated evidence of their attachment:

> *Dec 29th 1801* – We soon got into the main road and reached Mr Clarkson's at tea-time. . . .
> *Jan 24th 1802* – We had Mr Clarkson's turkey for dinner, the night before we broiled the gizzard and some mutton. . . .
> *Mar 11th 1802* – Just as we were sitting down to dinner we heard Mr Clarkson's voice. I ran down. William followed. He [Clarkson] was so finely mounted that William was more intent upon the horse than the rider, an offence easily forgiven for Mr Clarkson was as proud of it himself. We walked with him round by the White Bridge after dinner. . . . The vale in mist rather than the mountains, big with rain, soft and beautiful. Mr Clarkson was sleepy and soon went to bed.

When, because of Mrs Clarkson's failing health, the family was advised to leave the damp climate of the Lake District and return to East Anglia, Dorothy expressed her surprise that they had chosen Bury St Edmunds rather than London. She wrote to Catherine in June 1806:

> You might have lived more to your own satisfaction in London – you might have chosen your own society, and that of the best, and you need never have had more than you liked, which is not possible always in a country town.

Was she, I wonder, hinting that Catherine had given in too readily to her husband's preference for living in Suffolk? She need not have worried, because Catherine only wanted to be with her husband and was quite happy to retire to East Anglia rather than London.

However, it was fitting that the memorial plaque that was to be unveiled 150 years later in the Abbey, should have been cut from Cumbrian green slate and bear the simple inscription, *a friend to slaves*.

For the last thirty years of his life Thomas Clarkson lived quietly in the old moated house he now rented, known as Playford Hall. It would appear that he was now resigned to the knowledge that he would be seen as no more than a footnote in the annals of a century that had known both the best and the worst of human nature. During the last ten years of his retirement he had witnessed many events that were to change the future of Man's thoughts and actions. Charles Darwin was to challenge our concept of the Creation; Queen Victoria, at the age of eighteen, was to take over the throne of England; Charles Dickens was to expose the cruelty to children in this country and the evils of the workhouse system; Elizabeth Fry launched her organization called the Nursing Sisters; steam replaced sail for ships crossing the Atlantic; photography was invented; Sir Robert Peel was grudgingly accepted as the new Prime Minister; Wordsworth was elected Poet Laureate; women and children were at last banned from being made to work in coal-mines; the potato famine struck Ireland; and Parliament at last voted to reform the corn laws, thereby bringing about the downfall of Sir Robert Peel. Right up to the last year of his life Thomas Clarkson kept himself informed and continued to support the growing number of societies that were striving to improve the quality of life for men and women of all backgrounds and nationalities.

After a brief illness he died at the age of 86 and was buried in the churchyard at Playford. The obituaries he received in the national press and the tributes paid in most places of worship prove that Clarkson was not a man without honour at his death, and it may be that he has known oblivion for so long because his widow and Quaker friends did not, at the time, wish there to be any monument built to his memory. Wisbech, and other communities, though, could not allow this lack of public recognition to go on for long, and in 1880 the Gilbert Scott memorial was erected at a cost of £2,035*. But of what value is a monument unless it has been matched by deeds? A good man's actions should be enough for him to live in the memory. Sadly, our memories are often too short, or our minds too occupied with other things. In the end, it is proper that worthy men or women should have their names cut in stone if only to remind those who pass by that such worthy lives were lived.

---

* It was unveiled in 1881 by the then speaker of the House of Commons, the Rt Hon Bouverie Brand, MP, who, as the Liberal Member of Parliament for Cambridgeshire, was already well-known in the area.

Sir Gilbert Scott's memorial to Thomas Clarkson

I think you will understand now why I have devoted my last two letters to a very remarkable story. The other famous people of Wisbech that I mentioned in passing will have to wait until another day, which I am certain will come.

ᥴ᧐ 12 ᧐ᥩ

A Woman of Destiny

I don't know whether you would agree with me but I feel there are times when we oversimplify our heroes and heroines just as much as we often overromanticize them. I suppose it's natural, because we like the ingredients of a good story to have such dramatic opposites – rags to riches, local boy makes good, shy spinster outwits an empire, that sort of thing. It is being made to believe in the impossible. Maybe we feel we can identify more easily with people we think were ordinary and then share in their fairy-tale success. But the more biographies I read the more convinced I become that there are always latent qualities of courage or leadership in those who eventually, and often unwittingly, take on heroic status. There is, if you like, something already in the character that will separate such a person from the crowd, some strength that will manifest itself in action or achievement. This is not to lessen the stature of our hero or heroine – in some ways it can even increase it, especially if he or she, perhaps through privilege or background, had the choice to do other than what ultimately gave them their glory.

I have prolonged this thought at some length because I have just been reading a brief account of the life of Nurse Edith Cavell which I borrowed from a good friend and local historian, George Dixon. This brief biography, or lengthy tribute, was published by The Royal London Hospital to commemorate the 75th anniversary of the execution of Nurse Cavell and the 250th anniversary of the hospital in which she had trained. It is an attractive publication in French and English with several historic photographs, eight colour plates and sketches by Edith, who was also a gifted artist. From the camera portraits we have of her she was, in addition to all her other virtues, a lady of rare beauty, the beauty that comes from a very self-composed person who possesses both serenity and strength. To some people she appeared aloof and slightly detached from the earthly things going on around her. Her friends were few, but those who won her friendship received a quiet, deep affection that was constant. If she gave any personal love to anyone outside her family it was to her two dogs, Don and Jack.

The reason why I'm devoting a letter to this particular heroine is because I was recently asked to give a talk about some of the famous people connected with Peterborough, such as John Clare, Sir Malcolm Sargent, and several others who were pulled out from the drawers of history for the occasion. But the one person who appealed most to my small audience was Nurse Edith Cavell. This was not just because she had spent three years of her life in the city, from 1884 to 1887, but because of her outstanding contribution to nursing and, of course, her cruel and controversial execution which shocked the world.

Like many others, I was familiar with the bare bones of her story, and especially of her short time in Peterborough, when she was a student teacher at Miss Margaret Gibson's Private School in Laurel Court, next to the cathedral. Up until a few years ago there were still elderly ladies in Peterborough who had been pupils at that establishment and all had their own memories, either at first or second hand; one of them recalled that the headmistress, Miss Gibson, was not at all sure that Edith was cut out for the demanding career of a teacher. Perhaps, so the story goes, nursing would be more suitable. And so one built up a picture of this vicar's daughter, not all that academic or obedient, being sent off to boarding schools, never settling anywhere for long, a girl who was probably lonely, unhappy, and who became a nurse only to be shot in the First World War on a trumped-up charge of spying.

You see what I mean by oversimplifying the scenario? Some of what we hear is true, but it is paper-thin truth. The reality puts on many more skins and offers explanations which are necessary if we are to have a deeper understanding of her life.

Peterborough's claim to a share in the history of this remarkable woman is justified because it is possible that, without the advice, influence and help of Miss Gibson, she would not have gone into nursing in the first place. In any case that was not in fact her immediate choice, nor the career recommended by her headmistress. As so often happens, her destiny seemed to weave itself from chance or coincidence.

It was on this subject of destiny that the group of ladies to whom I was talking got involved in their own discussion. One ninety-two-year-old from Scotland (who didn't look a day over seventy) said that we make our own destiny, usually through our own mistakes. Another said that we had no say in what happened to us, we were simply caught up in the flow of events and made the best of it. Someone suggested that Edith Cavell could have accepted the advice of her superiors and left Belgium before it was too late, that in some way she contributed to her own martyrdom. One lady from Maidstone reminded me that Edith Cavell had worked there, which is true. (There are several other towns with which she is associated – Norwich, Clevedon, Steeple Bumpstead, London, Manchester and, of course, Brussels.)

It took a little time to restore order to my enthusiastic audience, and now that so many aspects of Nurse Cavell's life have been introduced into this letter I ought, for your sake, to go back to the beginning. Edith Cavell was born on 4 December 1865 in the Norfolk village of Swardeston, the eldest daughter of the Reverend Frederick Cavell and his wife Louisa Sophia. Eventually the vicarage was to become the home of three more children: Florence, Lilian and John. All the children were educated at home by their parents until they were ready for sending off to boarding school. For Edith that day came when she was fourteen years old and already proficient in most subjects, with a particular talent for drawing and painting. She was sent to Belgrave School, Clevedon, in Somerset, where she was seen as a very strong-minded student who did not care to mix much with the other girls. After a short time there her parents transferred her to Kensington, where her natural gift for the French language was recognized and encouraged. She was to receive the same opportunities when she moved to Peterborough in 1884. Miss Gibson saw in her eighteen-year-old student teacher a girl of unusual qualities, which did not necessarily include those necessary for the teaching profession. She believed that Edith was better suited for a career as a governess and, through her own connections with people in the right places, found an ideal post for her with a wealthy family in Steeple Bumpstead, Essex.

Although Edith's stay in Peterborough was a fraction under three years, I still like to think of her attending Evensong regularly in the cathedral and walking through the cloisters and the precincts on her way to shop in the then old market town. It was a very different city a hundred years ago, a city still coming to terms with the railways and industrialization. Agriculture was still important, as were the small family businesses that lined the streets. It was a city on the edge of the Fens but not of the Fens. Its county was then Northamptonshire; later it was moved into Huntingdonshire; now it is Cambridgeshire. Rather like a child moved from one foster home to another it didn't really know where it belonged, and for a time had no real identity; Charles Dickens once referred to it as 'the backdoor to somewhere else'. It is perhaps only now, with its expansion almost complete and the twentieth century nearly over, that Peterborough is beginning to mean something to people who live elsewhere and come here to shop. Edith Cavell would probably be mildly amused to know that the modern Queensgate shopping centre named one of its car-parks after her; she would, I am sure, be more grateful to know that the city's main hospital has paid her a better and more appropriate honour. There is also a dignified memorial tablet in Peterborough Cathedral, above a smaller one to her former headmistress, Miss Margaret Gibson. Further away, in London, is the most impressive monument of them all: the fine statue which stands in St Martin's Place, just off Trafalgar Square.

Edith left the Laurel Court School in 1887 to take up the position of governess which Miss Gibson had acquired for her in Steeple Bumpstead. This appointment was not going to claim many years of her life either. Having inherited a sum of money from a close relative she was able to indulge her passion for travel, especially on the Continent. Miss Gibson, who was to remain a friend, had now recommended her as a governess to the François family in Belgium, and, after her long holiday abroad, Edith knew it was an opportunity she could not decline. Her teaching would be restricted to four children, and she would be able to use her two languages and paint. They were to be five happy years but, again, this interlude was destined to be briefer than she would have wished. In 1895 her father was taken seriously ill and, as the eldest daughter, Edith saw it as her responsibility to return home immediately to Norfolk to nurse him.

She was obviously as good at nursing as she was at most things, because her father made a complete recovery. And it was *that* experience which made her realize where her true vocation lay. She now had a strong conviction that she had been called to heal the sick. At the age of thirty she was accepted as a nurse-probationer at The London Hospital, Whitechapel. After her six weeks' preliminary training the Matron, Miss Eva Luckes, felt much the same about her

Nurse Edith Cavell

as her former employers had done. She wrote in her register that Edith's 'self-sufficiency was one that was to impress all who met her and was to appear at times as aloofness, even abruptness'. She found, as others were to find, that it was not easy to become a close friend of Miss Cavell. Yet there was little reservation about her skills or care of patients. For that she was always admired.

Edith was soon working day and night shifts in the surgical and fever wards, seeing disease, poverty and suffering at first hand. However, the Matron still felt she was not in the right place or totally committed to being a ward nurse, so she transferred her for a year to the private nursing staff; this consisted of qualified nurses who were engaged to care for patients who could afford treatment in their own homes – usually middle-class families who were not prepared to go into public hospitals. Then, in 1899, Edith was offered the post of Night Superintendent at the St Pancras Infirmary, and accepted.

You can see how many extra pieces there are to the jigsaw puzzle if we are to get a complete picture. After three years at her St Pancras job, which she did not like, she applied for and was appointed to the post of Assistant Matron at Shoreditch Infirmary. To some employers she would have been seen as a bit of a flitter, never staying in one job for more than two or three years; to others she was seen as a woman gaining experience in all fields of medicine and ambitious to put it into practice. Her great aim now was to train probationers to become better nurses and to reorganize hospital procedure.

After a temporary appointment as head of Queen's District Nurses in Manchester came the offer of an appointment that was to change the course of her life completely. In 1907 she was invited to become the Matron of a training school for nurses in Brussels, having been highly recommended by the François family for whom she had worked as a governess before her father's illness. Her superior was the famous Dr Antoine Depage, a married man of forty-five, who later became president of the Belgian Red Cross. He was anxious to improve the standard of nursing in Belgium, which had been very much in the hands of religious communities. He also believed that the best-trained nurses came from England and was happy to accept the François' suggestion that Edith should be put in charge.

But in three years' time there was to be yet another change, another promotion. Edith was given her own hospital, the new, large secular hospital of St Gilles in the expanding suburbs of Brussels, which had modern wards, well-equipped operating theatres and a spacious out-patients department. She had arrived. It was 1910, and, despite some opposition to her working methods, the future looked promising. It was to do so for only four more years.

In 1914 came the moment that changed more than the history of one woman – but it was her involvement in the first eighteen months of that most tragic war that was to bring about an end to

her career. It all started innocently enough. She was only doing
what she thought a nurse should be doing for wounded men. But
she was no ordinary nurse, and for her just healing the sick was not
enough. She had to save these men from further bloodshed and, if
possible, get them home. What began as an act of mercy ended up
as an organized escape story of classic proportions.

In 1915 the Germans took over her hospital at St Gilles and
staffed it themselves. Edith refused to register with the occupying
authorities and became increasingly involved in the resistance
movement, helping hundreds of British and allied soldiers to
escape. It was a dangerous and complex operation but, because
Edith was still allowed to run the training school for nurses at
Ixelles, she felt she had sufficient protection to continue her under-
ground activities on the grounds of compassion. Some of her
colleagues and close acquaintances questioned her wisdom in doing
so, and even suggested she should return to England. Was it wise,
prudent or morally right for an English nurse, in a position of some
authority in a foreign country, to use her professional immunity as
a cover for her patriotic or humanitarian convictions?

It did not take long for the German secret police to discover
where the main escape route was and who was organizing it. Edith
was warned of their surveillance but still refused to turn away the
growing number of soldiers who were now coming to her, either
wounded or as escaped prisoners of war. The secret police watched
patiently for three months, gathering information, building up their
case, trying to discover the full extent of the operations and Nurse
Cavell's activities, which they decided also included spying.

On 31 July her associate, Philippe Baucq, was arrested. Five days
later they came for her. She was interrogated until 10 August, when
she was taken to St Gilles prison, close to the hospital which she
had helped to establish. Several other members of the organization
were also taken into custody, accused with Edith of crimes against
Germany. Their trial began on 6 October 1915. It was a very one-
sided affair, and Edith soon knew what the outcome would be. On
10 October she sat in her cell and wrote a letter to her nurses,
thanking them for what they had achieved for medicine in eight
years and also reminding them of their duty to continue the work
she had started.

On 11 October the military tribunal announced its verdict. Five
of the conspirators were sentenced to death, with the sentences on
Philippe Baucq and Nurse Cavell to be carried out immediately. The

news caused worldwide outrage and condemnation. Britain, Belgium, France and America all tried to prove that Edith was neither a traitor nor a spy. But the German military power naturally remained insensitive to their criticism and unmerciful in the face of all pleas for clemency.

At dawn the following morning Edith Cavell was led out into a courtyard to face a firing squad. The self-composure and strength which she had shown all her life were to sustain her even in this most dreadful moment. The night before she had said:

> I have no fear or shrinkage. I have seen death so often that it is not fearful or strange to me; and this I would say, standing as I do in view of God and Eternity, I realise that patriotism is not enough. I must have no hatred or bitterness against anyone.

It is not often in history that those forgiving words have been heard just before an execution. I can think of one other occasion, but that was nearly two thousand years ago.

The doctor who was ordered to be present at her death said that she was the bravest woman he ever met. 'She went to her death with a poise and a bearing which it is quite impossible to forget.' It was all a far cry from the quiet precincts and cloisters of Peterborough Cathedral, a far cry from the stern but compassionate Miss Gibson, who must have wondered at the time what would become of her talented but strong-headed pupil.

When the world heard that the execution had taken place, Germany was condemned as a brutal nation for killing a woman whom everyone else believed to be an 'angel of mercy'. To shoot a woman and a nurse in cold blood was barbaric. Germany tried to justify its action, but there were few who wanted to listen.

There are, of course, still many questions left unanswered, which brings me back to the point I was making at the beginning of this letter (which I certainly did not mean to be quite so long). It is always a risky business oversimplifying, or even romanticizing, our heroes and heroines. What motivates a person to behave in a particular way, even against the odds, is something peculiar to the human race.

There is just one more episode in the story of Edith Cavell which I would like to leave with you. When the First World War was over it was decided to move her body from its grave in Belgium for reburial in Britain. It was a sombre occasion of great ceremony, with

George V, Queen Mary, Albert King of the Belgians and many other dignitaries present. The body was escorted by men of the Royal Navy and Belgian Army to Dover, then to Westminster Abbey for a funeral service, and finally to Norwich for the last burial. It was reported later that when her body was exhumed death had not defamed her or robbed her of her beauty. Her hands still held the Prayer Book which was buried with her, inscribed with the words 'Died at 7 a.m., October 12th 1915. With love to my Mother – E. Cavell'.

It would indeed be impossible to forget so great and noble a lady, and by the time my talk with my group was over we all felt she had been touched by destiny, whether of her own making or not.

৩ 13 ৩

Ghosts and Silver Ghosts

How many people, I wonder, realize as they drive up or down the A1 between Wansford and Norman Cross, that they are only a stone's throw from the birthplace of the man who gave the world one of its greatest cars, which was to become synonymous with engineering perfection?

I refer, as if you hadn't already guessed, to the famous Rolls-Royce and its creator Frederick Henry Royce, who was born in the miller's house at Alwalton, a peaceful village just off what was once the Great North Road in what was then the county of Huntingdonshire. Now it is in Cambridgeshire, and the old part of the village lies hidden like a bird's nest in a cluster of trees which protect it from the ceaseless throb of traffic going north and south.

The house in which this engineering genius was born on 27 March 1863 is no longer there, and I was told only the other day that when it was pulled down the stones went to build the mill-house at nearby Castor. The village itself has inevitably changed quite a lot in the past hundred years but it is there where this story of determination and success begins and, to some extent, ends.

The boy's father, James Royce, came from a fairly successful family of millers and farmers in the north of England. If not exactly the black sheep of the family, he does appear to have been stubborn and irresponsible. By getting well away from the family influence James planned to run his own business as a miller at Alwalton. However, because of ill health, the fragile state of the agricultural economy and his own unsteady temperament, he was not to enjoy the success or prosperity he hoped would be his by branching out alone.

In 1867, when Frederick Henry was only four years old, his father decided to sell up and move to London, where he believed that life would be kinder to them. It wasn't. James Royce died five years later, a sad and ruined man. Consequently, his wife had to find work as a housekeeper to earn what money she could for her children – Emily, born 1853; Fanny, born 1854; Mary, born 1856; James, born 1857; and Frederick, born 1863. It was a familiar story. Several children in quick succession and the mother suddenly widowed, with no money and little strength left for the extra work that now had to be done to provide them with food.

Later in his life Sir Henry (as he became) was to tell a friend that 'my food for the day was often but two slices of bread soaked in milk'. It was a lonely and at times miserable childhood. Even before moving to London he had known what it was to be sent out as a small boy to scare the birds off the land for sixpence a week. In London he turned his attention to wheels, to anything that revolved, and soon became fascinated by railway engines and the locomotive machinery to be found at the main-line stations. To supplement his mother's earnings he took a job as a newsboy, selling papers for W H Smith at Clapham Junction and Bishopsgate. (He was to do this also on the streets of Peterborough, when he returned a few years later to become an engineering apprentice.)

Like his father, he did not enjoy good health, and his insistence on hard work ultimately demanded compromise. He also received very little formal education but was to become another example of what can be achieved by someone who was mainly self-taught. By the time he was a young man he had acquired a sound knowledge of algebra, electrical currents, astronomy and some foreign languages. Later he became interested in art and was a competent artist. When asked how he had managed to learn so much he replied that he was blessed with a very retentive memory, and consequently hardly forgot anything he read or heard.

It sounds a success story that is almost too good to be true, but it has to be said that there were to be many changes of fortune between those early days of struggle and the emergence of Henry Royce as a cultured man and a baronet. At the age of thirteen he became a telegraph boy, and a year later he obtained an apprenticeship with the Great Northern Railway at their locomotive engine works and repair sheds in Peterborough. For this privilege he had to pay £20 a year, the money for which was provided by an aunt who looked upon him as her favourite nephew. He took lodgings in the city with an elderly couple who had been friends of his father in Alwalton.

Peterborough in those days was still a relatively quiet and grey city with a mixture of ecclesiastical and agricultural interests trying to keep the industrial revolution at bay. But the railways had arrived, and industry was waiting at the city gates; soon there were to be several important engineering works which would dominate the growth of the area for years to come. But for a fourteen-year-old boy segregated from his family in London it must have been a lonely place.

Henry stayed at this menial job until he was seventeen, acquiring, as he said later, some skill as a mechanic but lacking technical experience. When told by his beneficent aunt that she could no longer afford the £20 a year to continue his apprenticeship, he decided to go north in search of employment, possibly as an unqualified tool-maker. It was not easy. Because of the industrial depression of the late 1870s there were men with far more experience looking for work. He eventually found a job in Leeds, working fifty-four hours a week for eleven shillings (the equivalent of 55p today).

Realizing that he desperately needed further qualifications if he was to advance beyond being a lowly-paid labourer, he returned to London to attend lectures given by the eminent Professor Ayrton at Finsbury Polytechnic, and to take some examinations. This enabled him in 1883 to apply for and get a job with the Electric Light and Power Company in Liverpool, where, still only twenty years old, he was made responsible for the new street-lighting of that great city. To prove that he was worthy of this appointment he often worked eighteen hours a day, impressing everyone with his calm efficiency and gifts of organization, but with no thought for his health.

Even this was not a job for life, though, and his great dream was to own and run a business that would give him more scope and independence. Remembering what he had learnt in Peterborough, he began manufacturing small electrical devices of his own design, specializing in a dynamo that could be adapted for a variety of uses. In 1884 he went into partnership with a man named Claremont, and ten years later founded the company of F H Royce and Co., with a factory in Manchester. Success was on its way.

In 1893 he felt sufficiently established to get married and build a new house in Knutsford, Cheshire. One of the proud features of his new home was the garden, which displayed all his ideas of elegance and perfection. He was especially enthusiastic about his roses and fruit trees. What might seem strange to us now is that he did not consider it necessary to have a garage. His newly acquired car, which was French, was very much a workhorse, and he was not at all happy about the noise it made.

His production of a new dynamo was just beginning to prove successful when the British market collapsed under a flood of cheaper imports from Germany and America. Not to be beaten, he decided to turn his attention to the motor car, believing that with good design and skilled engineering it would be possible to produce an almost silent engine, creating a car that whispered instead of roared.

His first two-cylinder, ten-horsepower engine was ready for testing in April 1904 and was eventually shown to the young man who was to become his partner, the Hon. Charles Rolls, who was already an important name in motoring and the winner of the Automobile Club's Thousand Mile Trial in 1900. Charles Rolls was so impressed by Royce's design and the car's performance that by 1906 the two men agreed to join forces. Royce was the engineer and perfectionist with ideas, Rolls the competitive sportsman and wealthy backer with the money. Together they would create a car that was destined to become a legend.

But there was something else that was needed to make the Rolls-Royce car distinctive. After all, few people could actually see what went on underneath the bonnet. The bodywork had to match the engine, and the man who was to be responsible for this was Claude Johnson. He engaged well-known coach-builders, such as Barker, Hooper or Mulliner, who were charged with completing the image of excellence.

By 1906 a new Rolls-Royce was ready for the London Motor Show. It now had a completely new six-cylinder 40/50-horsepower engine, with a 7428-cc capacity. When the bodywork received its aluminium paint, and the metalwork was silver-plated, there was only one name to give this almost silent and stunning revelation – the Silver Ghost. It amazed the motoring world and was to remain in full production for almost twenty years, surpassing in popularity its greatest rival at that time, the Mercedes.

Claude Johnson was a practical businessman who believed that the most important selling feature of the car was its reliability. To prove that the Silver Ghost was the best car being made anywhere in the world he put it through many demanding test trials, including sending it on a non-stop tour of Britain. The engine ran for 14,371 miles without a hiccup, beating the previous record by a considerable distance.

The Rolls-Royce was now universally accepted as the symbol of perfection, and it was in demand by royal families and state leaders throughout every continent. The Silver Ghost was seen in Paris, Brussels, Berlin and Budapest, and then America. It was a sensation. To meet the resulting demand a new factory was established in Derby, the town which was to become the future home of all Rolls-Royce engines for the next fifty years.

Sadly, the Hon. Charles Rolls, who had shown so much faith in Royce's genius, did not live long enough to see how famous their creation would become. In July 1910 he was killed in a flying accident, aged thirty-two – the first aviation casualty in this country. In the same year Henry Royce's own health broke down again, and his doctors prescribed a complete rest, preferably near the sea. Hearing that idleness was the remedy was not easy to accept, but he decided to move to Overstrand, near Cromer in the hope that he would soon recover. But Norfolk was not always as warm as he would have wished, and in the end he decided to accept Claude Johnson's advice and buy a small villa near the village of Le Cannadel in the south of France. He moved his English home to Sussex, finally settling at West Wittering, where he was to die in 1933.

Neither ill-health nor retirement could force Henry Royce into idleness or obscurity, though. He was still only forty years old, and there were many plans he wanted to see fulfilled before old age took over. In both his French and Sussex homes he had rooms converted into drawing-offices and invited his chief designers from Derby to come and work with him on new ideas in these conducive surroundings. One suggestion was that the classic design of the Rolls-Royce cars still needed another distinguishing feature – something that no one else could copy. The R-R logo in red letters was already familiar, so Royce commissioned the artist Charles Sykes to create a mascot to go on the radiator. The result was the daring, wind-swept *Spirit of Ecstasy*, for which the artist is said to have used the attractive secretary to Lord Montagu of Beaulieu as his model.

The R-R monogram continued to be finished in red until 1933, when it changed to black. Some accounts have suggested that this was done as a tribute to Henry Royce, who died that year, but the decision to change was made months before he died. Other accounts say that the colour was changed because the Duke of Kent criticized the manufacturers for using the revolutionary colour of

Communism. Maybe he did, but the truth is that the firm was having difficulty in getting red enamel to adhere to the newly introduced material chromium plate; black was the only colour it would take, so there was no other choice. As so often happens in life, reality was far less romantic than fantasy.

By the second decade of the century, having created the nearest thing to perfection in cars (at least for the time being), Henry Royce was hungry for a new challenge, and so turned his attention to the aviation industry, which was the latest unconquered summit in engineering. In 1914 his ideas received an unexpected impetus with the declaration of the First World War and the Government's demands for more planes, not only for reconnaissance but for combat; bomb-dropping was to come later. Speed was the first requirement. Royce had developed a twelve-cylinder, water-cooled engine and was able to go into mass-production as soon as orders were received. The Eagle, as he called his new brainchild, was ready for flying a year later, and this was followed by the Hawk, the Falcon, the Condor and the Kestrel. By the end of that war seventy-five per cent of British aircraft were using Royce engines.

Car production had now taken second-place. Even so, developments were progressing there, too. Engines were designed to be more powerful and economical. By 1925 a new model was unveiled, partly to take the place of the Silver Ghost – though that was still to remain a collector's item. The new Phantom I had a 7.6-litre, six-cylinder engine and also introduced front-wheel braking. It had a top speed of 90 m.p.h. It was followed by the Phantom II (1929) and Phantom III (1932), each of which was to be *the* car chosen for ceremonial occasions.

In recognition of his services to aviation and the car industry Henry Royce, the poor boy from Alwalton, was made a baronet in 1930 and went on to become a famous personality throughout the world, especially in America, where the car industry was big business. By the time he had settled for good in West Wittering his wife had died, and he now relied very much on a gentle, considerate housekeeper to run his home and to look after his many guests. During these years he was able to spend more time with his other loves – gardening, painting and reading (particularly poetry and biography). His friends saw him still as a quiet, modest man with a benevolent attitude towards all who worked for him. Remembering some of the harsh employers for whom he had worked as a boy, and the blatant exploitation of unskilled labourers, he always tried to improve the conditions of his workers and be fair to them. In return he received loyalty and affection.

Perhaps it is worth recalling, if only to make the man sound human, that the only irritation he was known to show in these last years was caused by the public, in those confounded new motor cars now coming off the mass-production lines, invading Sussex to spoil some of his favourite and most secluded spots. Maybe it was not so much the cars that annoyed him as their owners and their noisy behaviour. The situation has not improved (there is a debit side to everything that is invented to give us a so-called better life).

A few months before his death on 22 April 1933, Sir Henry had already started work on the Merlin engine, which was later to power the Spitfire and Hurricane fighters in the Second World War. His concept of engineering as an art had been imbued in all his staff, many of whom he had trained personally. After his death, now led by A G Elliot, they were able to carry his ideas through even into those post-war years when Rolls-Royce engines were used in such aircraft as the Viscount, Comet and later the Boeing 707.

All this was an incredible achievement for a man who had once earned sixpence a week scaring birds before he could read, and who sold newspapers on the streets of London before he started work as an unskilled apprentice. At his death his colleagues and friends could not find words adequate to praise him. He was described as 'one of nature's gentlemen' and 'the kindest man to work for'. Patrick Murphy, writing in the *Sunday Express* at the time of his death, said of him: 'Of all the great men I have met he was the simplest and most charming.'

Henry Royce, who was never ashamed to go back to the scenes of his beginnings or to talk about his early struggles, did not see himself as a genius. He maintained that his designs were really quite simple and mostly the offspring of commonsense. They were successful because he found gifted engineers to put them into practice. But what those engineers knew was that he too had been a good craftsman, and he respected their skill. He was never happier than when he was on the shop floor in his overalls, covered in oil and grease. He loved engines as some men love horses, fishing, or golf.

By today's standards he was not a wealthy man, not a get-rich-quick millionaire with a life-style to match. He was just grateful that his success had given him comfort for his last years, a house with a beautiful garden, and friends who enjoyed his quiet company. In his will he left £112,598, which was distributed among many of those friends and the good causes he supported, including £11,000 to research to try to find a cure for the common cold and influenza. Royce had frequently commented that these minor ailments caused British industry the loss of more working hours than anything else, and he believed that in time a remedy would be discovered. Well, as we know, so far it hasn't happened, and it may well have been the one thing that would have disappointed him had he lived for another fifty years.

The success of Henry Royce's original dream and creation was to continue long after his death. The Silver Ghost was followed by the Silver Dawn in 1949; the Silver Cloud followed in 1955, with later models in 1959 and 1962. In between the Phantoms and the Silver Clouds had come the Wraith – cars of luxury and excellence, with air-conditioning and cocktail cabinets, as well as speed and reliability. Then came the Silver Shadow in 1965 and the Silver Spirit in 1980. Yet, in a way, they were all to become ghosts haunting an age of grandeur and wealth that symbolized for most the unattainable. When the Silver Cloud was road-tested in 1955 the *Autocar* magazine said of it 'at 60 mph the loudest noise in the new Rolls-Royce comes from the electric clock', and one knows that now even that would have been eliminated.

After his funeral service and cremation in Sussex, Henry Royce's ashes were taken to Derby, the home of the Rolls-Royce engines. There they were to remain until the outbreak of the Second World War, when they were moved for safety to the parish church of St Andrew at Alwalton, the village where his life had started so unpropitiously seventy years earlier. I spent a very pleasant hour there only a few days ago, walking down to the stream that feeds into the River Nene, a path he must have known. The rush of water through the sluice-gates muted any noise of traffic from the A1. The path was bordered by tall nettles, thistles and teasels. Sleek terns dived and skimmed over the water. A narrow boat was being manoeuvred through the lock. Two young men were fishing. It was as peaceful a scene as one could wish for, and one could understand why it always had a special place in the affections of Henry Royce.

Now, like Edith Cavell, he has a car-park in Peterborough named after him, which is at least marginally more appropriate for him than Nurse Cavell or John Clare. But when you have created something as immortal as the Silver Ghost and all its progeny, who needs a greater monument!

The church of St Andrew, Alwalton

P.S. Shortly after writing this letter I read in the national press that Rolls-Royce may soon cease to be a British institution: I do not think Sir Henry would be amused.

P.P.S. The latest news is that, after a long battle with BMW, it looks as if the new owners will be Volkswagen!

᥿ 14 ᥿

A Tale of Two Widows

I have been meaning to tell you for some time about a village on the edge of the Fens that has a particular fascination for me because of its associations with two women, from very different social backgrounds, who get into the history books because of the men they married. I am almost tempted to say, who had the ill-luck to marry the men they did, because both husbands met an end that neither wife would have wished even in their most sorely tested moments of marriage.

The two women were Elizabeth Cromwell, who was married to the Lord Protector, Oliver Cromwell, and Martha Clare, who was married to the poet John Clare. These two widows now lie, if not side by side, at least in close proximity within the consecrated grounds of Northborough church; one on the inside, the other on the outside.

Like most villages which are just off a busy major road, Northborough has changed greatly since those two ladies, at different times, lived there. Its history goes back even further than the first recorded mention in 670, when it was known as Norburgh; recent excavations in the area prove there were settlements there long before that. When the Clares moved to Northborough in 1832 it had a population of 230, which was considerably smaller than the 450 of Helpstone where Clare was born.

Now the new world has taken over from the old, and cars pass through the village streets with the regularity of a heartbeat. Fortunately for us, though, the houses in which our two widows spent their last years are still standing, and they, in themselves, illustrate the great gulf between their lives.

Without showing favouritism towards one or the other (as if I would), I will write of them in chronological order. Elizabeth

Bourchier married Oliver Cromwell a few months after his twenty-first birthday, on 22 August 1620, at St Giles's Church, Cripplegate, London. She was a wealthy, plump, round-faced woman, well-known for her thrifty housekeeping, who took great delight in collecting pictures of foreign royal families. She was tolerant of her husband's ambitions and only occasionally felt it necessary to chastise him for being away from home so often and for so long. That he loved her is beyond doubt. Even after they had been married for thirty-one years he was still able to write to her from Scotland:

> My Dearest, I could not satisfy to omit this post although I have not much to write; yet indeed I love to write to my dear, who is very much in my heart.

Elizabeth bore her husband eight children – four sons and four daughters. The Cromwells' connection with Northborough was established by the marriage of his favourite daughter – also named Elizabeth, but known as Bettie – to John Claypole. Cromwell was uneasy about the match because Claypole was known to be a bit of a rake, a wild, debauched and ungodly cavalier, but a brave soldier. His father (also John) was an old friend of the Protector and owned the fourteenth-century manor which had once belonged to Michael de Norburgh, Bishop of London. The manor and lands had been bought by the Fitzwilliams, who eventually sold the house and surrounding grounds to the Claypoles. Cromwell was to be a frequent visitor and relied on several influential families in the area for support.

Bettie was only sixteen when she married the young Claypole on 13 January 1646 in Holy Trinity Church, Ely, where her family then lived. Favourite daughter she might have been, but her father was too busy with his other duties to attend the wedding – either that or he did not want to give her away to a man whom he did not trust. The marriage was to last twelve years before Bettie was taken seriously ill with the cancer that was to end her life on 6 August 1658. In the June of that year she had already suffered her own grief when her youngest son, christened Oliver, died at the age of one. Her father was so broken-hearted at the death of his daughter that he collapsed and was unable to attend her funeral four days later.

There now comes a most extraordinary twist in the tale. Contrary to all expectations and loyalty to her father's beliefs,

Bettie had sympathized with the Royalists to such an extent that she pleaded with her father for the release of many who were then in prison. Unable to refuse his darling girl anything she asked, he pardoned scores who had been condemned to death. Was it because of this that Bettie was buried in Westminster Abbey, her body borne in stately solemnity down the Thames from Hampton Court to Westminster in a barge fit for a queen? One can imagine the scene on that calm summer evening, the mourners in their own barges draped in black, scattering petals on the water, the distant tolling of the Abbey bell, the cortège drifting silently as black swans to the mooring at Westminster, then the procession into the Abbey where Bettie was to be interred in the Henry VII Chapel. At least she was to lie in peace there for her eternity, the only member of the Cromwell family whose remains are still there.

Less than a month after Bettie's death Oliver Cromwell himself died. After a short period of lying in state he, too, was to be buried in the abbey, but not for long. With the restoration of the monarchy came also retribution. In 1661 his corpse – with those of two other Commonwealth supporters, Bradshaw and Ireton – was dragged through the streets of London to Tyburn. There all three were hung up for public ridicule. That ignominy complete, they were taken down, beheaded and mutilated, and each torso was thrown into a deep pit. The heads were kept for public display, stuck on poles near Westminster Hall, for the whole world to see what can become of those who outlive their ambitions, fame, triumphs and tyranny.

As for Lady Elizabeth, Cromwell's widow, fate was to prove more generous and sympathetic. Although she moved into St James's Palace for a few months after her husband's death (with an annuity of £20,000), she soon realized that it would be better to leave London. She considered both Wales and Switzerland as suitable places to get away from public censure and the world's affairs, but in the end chose to end her days in Northborough Manor, under the protection of her widowed son-in-law, John Claypole. And that is where, on 19 November 1665, she died, to be buried with some splendour in the family vault in the church of St Andrew.

It was not long before stories started circulating in the Fens about sightings of Cromwell's ghost, even at Northborough, but if all ghost stories were to be believed then our fields, lanes, churchyards, halls and houses would be over-active with hauntings.

The other widow of this tale, Martha Clare, is buried outside in the cold eastern corner of the churchyard, in a grave made bare by frost and wind. Even in summer the grass stays damp for most of the day with morning mist untouched by the sun. Martha, whom Clare always called Patty, presents us with a very different story. Born on 3 March 1799, Martha Turner was the daughter of a shepherd who lived at Walkherd Lodge, between Casterton and Pickworth. She was to earn her place in history by marrying a then unknown, penniless poet who was to be committed to a lunatic asylum for the last twenty-two years of his life.

Clare first saw Martha as she made her way home across the fields from Tickencote, a small village not far from Stamford, where on Saturday nights he played the fiddle in the local inn called the *Flower Pot*. He tells us in his autobiographical sketches that he fell in love with her at first sight, and was 'very ill at rest' until he found out who she was and whence she came. He climbed to the top of a pollarded tree to see which way she went, watched until she was out of sight and made up his mind to look for her again the following Saturday. He had to wait a few weeks before she appeared again, but when she did he lost no time in asking her if he could walk her home. She agreed, and so began what Clare described as 'some of the happiest & unhappiest days my life hath met with'.

Martha – or Patty as we must now call her – was an attractive young woman. She was, according to Clare's first biographer, Frederick Martin, a 'fair girl of eighteen, slender, with regular features and pretty blue eyes'. Spencer Hall, who visited her many years later at Northborough, said, 'she must have been a very comely girl in her day', and it is certain that Clare would not have courted any girl who was not physically attractive, even though she could neither read nor write.

Clare and Patty were married on 16 March 1820 in the church of Saints Peter and Paul, Great Casterton. The entry in the parish register is both moving and significant in its simplicity: under the relatively flowing signature of John Clare is the crude, shaky cross made by Patty as her mark. Clare was then twenty-seven and his wife twenty-one. As her father had also disapproved of the marriage and refused to attend the wedding, Patty was given away by her uncle John Turner. There was no honeymoon, not even the chance of living together to begin with. They had no spacious manor awaiting them. Patty returned to live with her parents, Clare with his. It was not until a few months later, when their first child was expected, that they were allowed to live together in the small cottage in Helpstone where Clare was born.

As with Elizabeth Cromwell, all the major events in Patty's life were concerned with her husband, who, for a few brief years, was to know his own summer of fame – mainly in London, where he became acquainted with many leading literary figures of his day, including William Wordsworth, Charles Lamb and Thomas De Quincey. However, I must remember that this letter is about Mrs Clare not her husband. I can do no more for him here than I attempted for Oliver Cromwell, to sketch in a few facts which will justify the purpose of this present narrative.

Clare, who never knew what it was to be free of financial worries, was frequently in debt both to the landlord of the *Blue Bell* in Helpston and to the landlord of their cottage. In 1832, much against his will, Clare accepted a cottage in Northborough which had been made available to them at a modest rent by the poet's life-long patron, Lord Fitzwilliam of Milton Hall. Compared with the Helpstone cottage it was spacious, with a large garden and orchard. Patty was excited at the prospect. At least she would be mistress in her own house and away from the village gossip she had put up with for the past twelve years. There was even enough land for them to keep a couple of pigs and maybe a cow (Clare's friends were already beginning to refer to him as 'farmer Clare' rather than 'poet Clare').

The flitting took place early one June morning in 1832. All their belongings were stacked on to a hand-cart and pushed along the field path from Helpstone to Northborough. At that hour of the day the great Fenland sky above them would have had a pale softness, one that Clare would have described as a 'gentle sky / Where not a cloud dares soil its heavenly light.' He may have noticed the skylarks singing, but my guess is that he was too miserable, too heavy-hearted to have noticed anything. Within hours of arriving at Northborough he was writing:

> I've left my own old home of homes
> Green fields and every pleasant place;
> The summer like a stranger comes
> I pause and hardly knew her face ...
> I sit me in my corner chair
> That seems to feel itself from home;
> I hear bird music here and there

From hawthorn hedge and orchard come,
I hear but all is strange and new.

Clare would never be able to come to terms with losing the security of his native village and, even more, of the countryside around it, which was his Eden, his world of unblemished innocence and joy. Yet, in the few years that he was to live in Northborough he wrote some of his finest poetry. However, his mental illness was now making life difficult for himself and his family. Little was known about the shadows of the mind in the nineteenth century, and Clare's problem was probably diagnosed as something far more serious than it was at that time. In 1837 he was taken to Dr Matthew Allen's private asylum at High Beech, Epping. Four years later he escaped and walked all the way back to Northborough, a distance of more than eighty miles. By the end of that year (1841) he was moved to the General Lunatic Asylum in Northampton, where he was to stay for the rest of his life. He died in 1864, aged seventy-one, largely forgotten by all but a few loyal readers. Had he not already foreseen this when he wrote:

I am – yet what I am, none cares or knows;
My friends forsake me like a memory lost.

During all those years Patty had the burden of running the house, of caring for the large garden and orchard, and of looking after her family, including Clare's father, who died there in 1846. She also received a few unwanted visitors, curious to know about the mad poet and any unpublished work – literary vultures in the main. In 1850 she was taken seriously ill and was threatened with eviction because of rent arrears. The only person who seemed capable of holding the family together now was her son Charles, who earned £4 a year as a solicitor's clerk in Market Deeping. But he died in 1852 at the age of nineteen and poor 'Widow Clare', as she became known prematurely, was left to survive as best she could. She has sometimes been criticized for not visiting her husband in the asylum, as if she did not care. But surely one can understand why it was an almost impossible task for her; apart from the expense of the journey itself she could not spare the time away from her family. Nor was it likely that Clare would have recognized her had she gone.

Patty did not know of her husband's death on 20 May 1864 until four days later, on 24 May, when he was due to be buried in Helpstone. The letter from the Northampton General Lunatic Asylum had gone astray. It was only because his body arrived too late for burial on the appointed afternoon that she and her family were able to get to Helpstone the day after. It had always been Clare's wish that he should be buried in his native village, and many stories have been embroidered about the night his body rested in the bar of the *Exeter Arms*, including the one about body-snatchers being engaged to cut out his brain so that London surgeons could further their investigations into the supposed relationship between madness and genius. Fortunately they did not succeed, and the funeral was able to proceed without further delay. It was reported in the *Stamford Mercury* on 3 June 1864 that the poet's widow 'wept as she spoke of the many good qualities of her dear departed husband and of the ardent love he had always shown her ere he was so mentally afflicted'.

The villagers of Northborough had always respected Patty, sympathizing with her in her troubles and admiring her for her willingness to help others. She took in mending and did baking for those who could no longer perform such tasks for themselves, and always carried a supply of home-made sweets in her apron pocket to give to the children she met on her rounds. practical, down-to-earth Martha – with no one now to call her Patty – still believed that life had to be got on with, otherwise she was defeated too.

But soon the long years of struggle took their toll. She was taken ill in 1871 and never recovered. Like the widow of Oliver Cromwell, her body was taken to Northborough Church for the funeral service and then the interment in the burial ground behind the east end of the building. So, should you ever visit that churchyard you will now be able to ponder on the two wives whose destinies were so different, but for whom the end of life's journey was very similar.

Is it too fanciful to believe that after all these years Elizabeth Cromwell and Martha Clare have bridged their differences – that under a gentle Fenland sky their ghosts might occasionally pause to pass the time of day, might even sigh and talk about their husbands and the days that could have been? I thought the idea worth the following lines:

> Whatever might pass between you now
>   under the cold grey stones,

or likelier still in the lark-sprung air,
  must prompt a smile
as you pause to exchange the time of day
  by a crumbling wall,
causing a stir in your widows' bones –
      Elizabeth Cromwell and Martha Clare.

No matter that one with modest pomp
  was laid to rest inside
the church, and one placed in a grave made bare
  by frost and wind.
All's equal now, these late years cannot tempt
  more doubts in the mind.
Like two old neighbours you can confide –
      Elizabeth Cromwell and Martha Clare.

You talk of your husbands, ill-fated men,
  drawn by a single flame,
who, far from the world's cruel eyes, would care
  for you and your
children with tenderness not always shown
  beyond love's closed door.
You, too, bore the burden of their fame –
      Elizabeth Cromwell and Martha Clare.

Each in your darkened heart felt the shame
  and loneliness that death
settles on wives when their cupboards are bare.
  So you grew old
with no one to talk to until ghosts came
  and you were compelled
to meet in the sky's unfettered breath –
      Elizabeth Cromwell and Martha Clare.

ᥰ 15 ᥰ

Seeking Refuge in the Fens

At the risk of confirming your growing suspicion that I am
becoming a necrophile, let me tell you about my latest visit to
a churchyard.

Although I have passed through the village of Wisbech St Mary
on countless occasions, I had never stopped to look at the church.
I was told it contained an unusual collection of artefacts donated by
the late Canon Mowbray Smith, a man of some means, well-bred,
well-travelled, and one who took his duties as a parish priest seriously. To this day people speak of his generosity and care towards
those who needed help, whether they went to church or not. Many
of them were not even sure at the time from whom that help came;
his good deeds were done quietly and not for self-glory.

I was disappointed, but not surprised, to find the church locked
and could find no notice saying where the key was kept. So I
strolled round the churchyard with its interesting assortment of old
and new headstones. Some of the older ones I assumed had been
removed to create more space, others were still huddled together in
that sturdy, Victorian cosiness that gave them durability.

It was then that I discovered a grave with a small granite cross on
which were carved four Russian names:

Vladimir Pestereff – born June 1870, died Sept 1959.
Vera Pestereff – born December 1876, died April 1934.
Natalie (nee Pestereff) Markham – born May 1907, died 1967.
Nicholas Pestereff –born July 1911, died May 1976.

It is not unusual to find foreign names in Fenland churchyards.
As I have mentioned before, many nationalities have sought refuge
in the Fens. During the seventeenth century a large number of

Walloons and Huguenots came here to escape religious persecution in their own countries. Dutch and Scottish prisoners who were enlisted to assist in fen drainage also settled in the new land they had helped to create, as did some of the French prisoners who were held at Norman Cross during the Napoleonic Wars. Similarly, in the twentieth century, Ukrainians, Germans, Poles, Italians and, more recently Asians, Chinese and Japanese, have come to add their own cultures to the ancient traditions of the Fens. And now I am able to extend that list by adding this Russian family I discovered in Wisbech St Mary.

Who were the Pestereffs, and how did they come to be buried in this quiet, local churchyard? It has not been an easy task finding even what little I know of their story so far, but it is worth passing it on because I am sure that one day there will be a sequel. In any case, I do not like unsolved mysteries.

Once again I sought the help of the Wisbech Society and, in its Annual Report of 1986, found an article written by two of the Pestereffs' own daughters when they were in their seventies. This was enough to make my research worthwhile.

The Pestereffs were casualties of the Bolshevik Revolution of 1917. Before that historic event they had been a highly respected family living on the southern steppes of Tsarist Russia. They owned a large, beautiful house with thousands of acres of virgin land. It was the Russia we associate with the novels of Tolstoy and Chekhov, extremely wealthy families living in great houses, entertaining lavishly, and relying for their servants and labourers on the masses of illiterate, meagrely-paid serfs. Tsar Nicholas II was on the throne. Born in 1868, son of Alexander III, he was a man who still believed in the divine right of kings. His arrogant and autocratic methods of government, encouraged by his ambitious wife, had already led to a brief war with Japan in 1904. That had ended with Russia's humiliating surrender and consequent unrest among her people. The first revolution a year later made Nicholas yield to demands for a representative assembly whilst retaining the absolute right to rule.

When the First World War began in 1914 he took command of all Russian forces, leaving his headstrong wife Alexandra to govern in his absence. It was a disastrous arrangement. Influenced too much by that strange character Rasputin, she made mistake after mistake, and it is thought that her intolerant, eccentric behaviour hastened the Bolshevik Revolution of 1917, which was also to change the lives of the Pestereffs and, eventually, of all of us. As a result of that uprising the Russian monarchy was overthrown, and many of the aristocratic families were to go down with them, their properties and lands confiscated. In 1918 Nicholas and his family were assassinated. The rest is familiar history.

The Pestereffs were not politically involved, nor were they at all insensitive to the social problems around them. They loved music, literature and good company, but they also believed in improving the standard of living of all those who worked for them. Vladimir Pestereff, the father, made his fortune as a qualified mining engineer, and his wife Vera could be equally practical when it came to helping others as well as herself. As the events of 1917 dramatically unfolded they soon realized they would need far more help than they ever expected.

Fortunately, they had staying with them at that time an English lady – Miss Helen Clarke, who was related to the well-known family of Clarkes at Inham Hall, Wisbech St Mary. Helen was also engaged to the Rt. Hon. J H Whitley, who was then the Speaker of the House of Commons, whom she later married. Her own parents lived at Hunstanton, in Norfolk, and they were prepared to rent a house there for the Pestereffs if ways could be found of getting them to England. With connections in high places this was eventually made possible, but not before Miss Clarke and her Russian friends suffered great hardship at the hands of the Bolsheviks.

They finally reached England on 4 January 1921 – Vladimir and Vera Pestereff and their five children: Natalie, 14; Sophie, 12; Lisa, 10; Nicholas, 7; and Maroussia (Maria), 5. They went, as planned, to Hunstanton until more permanent arrangements could be made for them.

Like most refugees seeking asylum they brought with them only what they could carry. (One of the stories I was to hear in the village later was that Mrs Pestereff had sewn most of her jewellery inside the linings of her skirts and coat and was able to sell this to provide some capital for their immediate needs.) Because he was an immigrant Mr Pestereff was not allowed to take up employment in this country unless he could be totally self-sufficient. Miss Clarke turned for help to her brother in Wisbech St Mary, Mr J A Clarke, who suggested that Vladimir could do worse than try his hand at farming. If he could raise the money to buy a small plot of land, then it might be possible to arrange a post-war grant towards building a house. So, as Sophie and Lisa were to recall sixty-five years later: 'All possible valuables brought with us from Russia, including furs, jewellery, gold watches and chains, etc., were sold, and from the proceeds five acres of land were purchased in the parish of Wisbech St Mary.'

Until the house was built only Vladimir and his daughter Lisa came to stay with the Clarke family, and the rest remained in Hunstanton. With the assistance of one man, Mr Pestereff built a seven-roomed brick house on his plot of land, and by the spring of 1922 the whole family were reunited under one roof and able to recommence their life together. Soon they were growing fruit and vegetables, which they carted the three miles to Wisbech to sell on the market.

It was an enormous challenge to make good in a foreign country, especially in the 1920s, and their success is an incredible story of endurance, persistence and courage. Not only was Mr Pestereff having to get used to farming after being a mining engineer, his wife was having to adjust to the customs of English village life, and the children had to come to terms with receiving their education in English schools. All of them were to excel and distinguish themselves in their own ways. Sophie obtained her London University Matriculation Certificate; Nicholas became a qualified electrical engineer in Manchester; Natalie was to qualify as a State Registered Nurse and work at Addenbrooks Hospital in Cambridge; Lisa became a freelance artist before accepting a permanent appointment with Burall Brothers, printers; Maroussia qualified as a teacher and went to France for a year's language experience. All had earlier won scholarships to further their education and make these achievements possible.

With that kind of initiative and hard work the family soon became wholly integrated into the life of Wisbech St Mary, taking part in the religious and social life of the village to such an extent that Canon Mowbray Smith was soon asking Mrs Pestereff if she would organize the annual Christmas Party in the village hall and arrange some entertainment to stop the boys from fighting. Their daughters Sophie and Lisa remembered how 'for years afterwards we organized a Variety Show consisting of carols, dances, recitation and short plays – all in costume – lasting, with an interval, for about two hours'. These entertainments were so popular that they were repeated for the Womens' Institute. Mrs Pestereff was in fact a founder member of the local W.I., and Lisa was responsible for starting the Boy Scout group, becoming the first Scout Mistress on the understanding that she would always have a chaperone when they went camping.

Their individual stories would make a fascinating book, for they were to take their careers far beyond the Fens – Kenya, America, Scotland, and even the Isle of Wight. But soon tragedy was to change their lives again. Mrs Pestereff was diagnosed as having breast cancer and died in 1934; two of the children's marriages ended in divorce, and the Second World War meant that, because of their nationality, they were in a new kind of exile and not allowed to live within a certain distance of the coast. The family dispersed, and by 1943 the life of the Pestereffs of Wisbech St Mary had come to an end. Only the granite cross in the churchyard now marks where the ashes of four of them lie, and set me to discover what story lay behind that unusual memorial.

Surely there must be more articles about them somewhere, or someone who could remember them! Where did they live? What happened to the children? The Wisbech Museum and Public Library staffs were equally interested and helpful but could find no further trace of the family. Inquiries at the local papers also drew a blank, apart from an announcement in the Deaths column that Mrs Vera Pestereff had died on 7 April 1934. I began to feel it was time to give up my quest when I met my old friend Betty Spridgeon, the ex-Land Army girl who had told me why Gilbert White had visited the Fens in 1756. We both happened to be in the same bookshop in Peterborough for about two minutes and were both in a hurry. Had I not almost fallen over her wheelchair I might have missed her altogether. I quickly asked her if she could do some more detective work for me among the friends she had made in Thorney during those Second World War years. 'Leave it with me,' she said.

A few days later I heard from her. It so happened that one of the girls she had come to know in the 1940s had married an ex-prisoner-of-war who had been interned at the Thorney POW camp. Margaret and Fred Olesch now lived in Wisbech St Mary, and perhaps they would know something about the family of Russian refugees. Betty decided that it was time that she and her husband went to pay their friends a visit. She phoned me soon afterwards to say that she had tracked down a Mr Arthur Wing, who was eighty, and willing to talk to me on one condition – that I did not try to sell him any double-glazing. I liked his sense of humour and thought he sounded promising, so I phoned him and made an appointment.

I arrived early but he was already waiting for me outside his house, which is surrounded by acres of farmland, all of which had once belonged to his father, who died when Arthur was only three years old. 'I can't actually remember him,' he said, 'but I do recall my uncle lifting me up at the funeral so that I could drop my own little bunch of flowers on to my Dad's coffin.' With a memory like that I knew that he would be able to also remember something of the Pestereffs.

'Well,' he said, 'I didn't know them well, 'cus I were only an ol' boy at the time, but I do know that he kept a pig and goat in the garden, and maybe some hens. I used to go and pick raspberries and gooseberries for him, and strawberries. He was the first man I knew in the Fens to grow strawberries in tiers rather than on the ground. He was a big man with a bald head and a bit reserved, because I don't think he knew much English.'

I asked about Mrs Pestereff. 'She was a big lady, too, very tall and awesome. She could speak English quite well. They hadn't been here long before we realized that they were a bit higher up the ladder than what we were. You know as well as I do that some people have a way of making you feel like that.'

'What about the children?' I asked. 'Did they become involved in the life of the village?'

'Some of them did, at least for a while. They got scattered about a bit in one way and another, especially during the Second World War. One of them married one of the Smedley boys of Wisbech and then went abroad, and one of them taught here in the village school. I could show you the house where they lived, if you like.'

I told him I would like that very much, and immediately he went off to change his shoes. 'I'll come with you in your car and then walk back. My doctor tells me that I must walk at least half a mile a day and keep taking the whisky.'

As we drove towards the house in Station Road he noticed two sisters leaning over their front gate talking to another lady. 'Pull over,' he said. 'That's Doreen and Pam Dix. They will know something about the Pestereffs.'

They were two charming, friendly village ladies who were not only prepared to revive their own memories of the Russian family who had come to live as neighbours but also invited me into their house to see a photograph of Mrs Vera Pestereff and two of her daughters, Natalie and Maroussia.

'They all spoke good English,' said Doreen, 'and Mrs Pestereff was quite a lady. They were very devout people and went to church every Sunday. She always wore fine clothes, including a very large hat with a long ostrich feather. As children we used to look forward to their arrival in church. They were usually the last to arrive and walked down the aisle to their pew at the front as if they were royalty.'

The two sisters now started exchanging memories between themselves. 'Do you remember how Mrs Pestereff was always bowing or nodding her head in church, and as she did so this blooming great feather used to wave up and down like a cow's tail. It had us in stitches. It was a job to stop giggling 'cus every time she bowed the feather would start bouncing up and down again and set us off once more. But they were nice people, very hard-working, very kind to everybody. They had their sadnesses too, though.'

I looked more closely at the photograph of the group, or guild, of Wisbech St Mary ladies. It was quite easy to pick out the regal Vera Pestereff and her attractive daughters. At least I now had proof that they had existed and thanked Doreen and Pam for their kindness. Then Arthur and I returned to the car so that he could show me where the house was. 'That's it – that white house on the right. That is where they lived, where I used to go and pick strawberries and raspberries. My God, I'd almost forgotten all about it until you came. Seems such a long time ago now. When they lived here it was called The Shelter. Now, as you can see, it's called The White House. There have certainly been some changes in the village since them days.' And with that he got out of the car to walk his half mile back home, as his doctor had ordered.

I drove home wondering what would happen next. I did not have to wait long. By the end of the week I received a letter from the Dix sisters enclosing another photograph of Mrs Pestereff with the ladies guild and one of a crowd at some local event in 1933, with Mr Vladimir Pestereff standing there, hatless, tall and impressive. All the ladies wore hats, and some were looking at what looked like hymn-sheets. Was it a funeral perhaps? I wrote to Doreen and Pam to ask if they could tell me what the occasion was, and it turned out to be 'the opening ceremony of the New Room built at Wisbech St Mary Church of England School for Cookery and Woodwork classes – and other lessons!' What, I wondered, was Mr Pestereff thinking as he stood there, so far removed from the life he had once known in Russia, a land he was never to see again. He died in 1959, aged 89.

A few days later I received another letter from the Dixes enclosing a copy of an article written by one of the Pestereff daughters. It was very similar to the one I had read in the Wisbech Society report but did tell me a little more about what happened to the rest of the family. Lisa married Richard Robinson, who was Professor of Philosophy at Cornell University, and went to live in America. Maroussia married Tom Image but was divorced eighteen months later. Natalie went to work in London for the Thames River Patrol and saw active service with the 'little boats' in the evacuation of Dunkirk, but, as a Russian, could not continue to serve in the Navy when invasion seemed imminent. She joined her brother in Edinburgh to study Social Sciences at the University, gaining her BA degree two years later. After the war she returned to Wisbech as the Personnel Welfare Supervisor at the local canning factory, married a colleague, A W M Markham and then emigrated with him to Kenya. Sophie taught at boarding schools in Malvern and on the Isle of Wight before returning to work for the Cambridgeshire Elementary Teachers' Brigade in Wisbech St Mary until Christmas 1943, when she married Major Prince David Wacznadze and moved to Scotland.

Eventually The Shelter was sold, and the story of the Pestereff family in Wisbech St Mary came to an end. All that I have been able to find out still only amounts to fragments of a much greater saga which might be written by someone else one day. Even so, I hope you won't think that my stroll around the churchyard that evening was a waste of time. Its consequences have kept me absorbed for six months, and I still feel reluctant to let the story go.

◈ 16 ◈

On the Brink

I seldom take a friend or visitor to Wisbech for the first time without hearing a sudden exclamation of surprise, even of admiration, as they look across the muddy waters of the River Nene and get the first full view of that elegant row of houses on the North Brink.

I do not think any of my friends would say 'Wow!' or 'Hey! Look at that!', but I do hear impressive comparisons being made, such as 'It reminds me a bit of Amsterdam', or 'It looks like part of Bruges'. Well, almost! Amsterdam, of course, is on a far larger scale, and Bruges happens to be one of the loveliest cities in Europe, with its own North Brinks lined with chestnut trees, but I know what my friends mean, and one cannot deny there is a certain Dutch or Belgian influence about the local prospect of fine buildings which gives to Wisbech its own dignity.

I admired it again this morning as I drove over to meet Miss Christina Swaine who had agreed to talk to me about the Peckover family – a subject very close to her heart. It was that family who eventually gave its name to one of the most important buildings on the Brink: Peckover House, which now belongs to the National Trust. In fact, Wisbech has more than one strong connection with the Trust, which I will come to later.

However, even before telling you what I learned about the Peckovers, I have to say that I have never seen the River Nene higher than it was today, especially along that low section between Guyhirn and Wisbech town bridge. In places it was actually over the banks, which is not a common sight even in winter. I suppose I noticed it particularly this morning because of the news we have been getting over the last few days of the flooding in Poland and eastern Germany, where the River Oder has brought disaster to

Central Europe. We have known plenty of flooding in the Fens, but not even the epic drama of 1947 was on a scale to be compared with what is happening now on the Continent. With over a hundred people dead, tens of thousands of animals drowned and vast areas of farmland under water, damage is already being put at £13 billion or more. And still the river rises, and with the floods come pollution, disease, despair and homelessness. Soldiers and civilians can fill sandbags and reinforce the banks until they drop with exhaustion, but nature cannot easily be tamed when it is in that mood. As Charles Kingsley said of the Fenmen's efforts to hold back our unruly waters:

> No one has ever seen a fen-bank break without honouring the stern quiet temper which there is in these men ... fighting the brute powers of nature .... But a hundred spades, wielded by practised hands, cannot stop that trickle. The trickle becomes a rush, the rush a roaring waterfall. The dyke-top trembles – gives .... The men make efforts, but the bank will break.

So I don't suppose I should get overexcited about the River Nene overflowing its banks between Guyhirn and Wisbech in the middle of summer. Yet, insignificant though this may be today, it is still a reminder of what can happen in any lowlands when the water levels rise so dramatically – and the weather throughout the world this year appears to be behaving in a most eccentric way.

Fortunately the North Brink, although on the bank of the Nene, is sufficiently elevated not to be in danger of flooding, and today the houses, lit by the mellow sun of morning, looked as permanent as any houses can. Within a few moments I knew I would be driving along that famous promenade from where I would be able to look back and see the South Brink, which has never made any effort to compete.

I had not met Christina Swaine before and wondered how our first meeting would go. I have tremendous respect for anyone who can devote several years of his or her life to unravelling the mysteries of a family history with such enthusiasm and diligence. To write a biography of one person is demanding enough – as I found out when I wrote a life of John Clare – but to take on a whole family with its incredible diversity of talents, personalities and achievements, is close to masochism or idolatry. For Christina, of course, it is simply a labour of love: she is not even sure that her work will be published, but it has to be written. By the end of the morning I felt she had almost become a member of the Peckover family.

Like many love affairs it began accidentally, though, as I have said before, I am not sure that I really believe in accidents. Prompted by none other than Dr Peter Cave, Christina started looking into the background of the Peckovers and their house on North Brink. That house, which was known as Bank House in their day, will always be associated with them, even though there were previous owners and the property is now in the hands of the National Trust (which, in 1998 will be celebrating the Golden Jubilee of its ownership) but news of that later. Having gone to Wisbech to find out more about the house, I soon found myself caught up in what can only be called a Fenland saga of banking, marriage, philanthropy, politics and Quakerism.

I think I should say that I was not totally unfamiliar with the Peckover dynasty, nor am I a stranger to the house. Over the years I have given several lectures or readings there, and have taken part in recitals. But they were passing associations, and I knew that for the purpose of this letter I would feel safer in the hands of someone for whom the subject was more than a casual interest. The story of the Peckovers is complicated enough anyway. The family history alone covers more than three hundred years – and it was a large family too. All I can be concerned with in this letter is that period which I will call 'the Wisbech connection'.

The first Peckover to move from Norfolk to Wisbech, in 1777, was Jonathan, who was then twenty-two years old. He opened a general store in the High Street and was obviously a young man with a natural flair for business. He had no doubt done plenty of research before deciding on Wisbech, where there were many Quakers. Because of his own religion Jonathan was able to attract most of the local Friends as his customers, and he in turn was soon to become a prominent member of their meetings.

He had been in Wisbech only four years when he decided to start a literary society. Such societies in those days often included the arts and sciences, as did the Spalding Gentlemen's Society, about which I wrote to you in an earlier letter. They usually began as discussion groups in the homes of the founders, then moved to larger premises as their membership grew. Jonathan Peckover's literary society was to be the acorn from which eventually, through his sons, grew the excellent Wisbech and Fenland Museum which is still thriving today.

Because he was a man to be trusted, it was not long before

people doing business in Wisbech, especially on market days, were asking him to look after their money for them. The Fens were dangerous places in the eighteenth and nineteenth centuries, as we can learn from the diary of John Peck, the Parson Drove farmer who, as the parish constable, saw plenty of lawlessness. He recalled the story of four Irishmen who had murdered William Marriott in Wisbech Fen in July 1795; they were executed at Wisbech on 24 October. Two of the condemned men were hanged in chains at Guyhirn, opposite where the murder was committed. And on 23 May 1819, he wrote:

> Abed by 10 o'clock. Called up immediately to apprehend two men on suspicion of robbing and ill-treating Arthur Ward, a cottager living by himself on Thorney Fen.

So in Jonathan Peckover's day it is quite certain that farmers returning to remote farms with their pouches full of money, were at risk. Highwaymen and robbers knew the area very well and were not slow to use brute force. The farmers felt that for a small fee it would be better to leave their gold in a strong safe in town. They were given a receipt, or promissory note, for whatever sum they deposited, which also gave them a guarantee to conduct other business transactions in the Fens. In other words, a local banking system was established, and by 1782 Jonathan Peckover was soon making a better living at that than he was in his own shop. It was clearly the way forward.

However, realizing that the world of finance was full of possible pitfalls and disasters, depending on trade and the country's economy, he decided to provide himself and his customers with a safety net by going into partnership with other established bankers. He now became an agent for Gurneys Bank at King's Lynn. Then, ten years later, he created his own bank, known as the Wisbech and Lincolnshire Bank, whilst still remaining a partner in Gurneys. This made sure that if he saw a crisis coming he was able to avert any threat to his own customers, or a run on the money invested with him. Unlike many men who entered banking, Jonathan Peckover had a wise head on his young shoulders.

Five years later, in 1787, Jonathan married Susanna Payne from Yorkshire, and eventually they started their own family. Although one of their three sons was to die in infancy, they decided in 1794 that it was time to move to a much larger house. As the most successful businessman in town, where else should he move to but the best house on North Brink? This spacious, three-storey house had been built in 1722. In 1752 it was bought by the Southwell family who lived there until 1794, when Jonathan became its new owner. In his day it quickly became known as Bank House, for obvious reasons. In no time at all he added a new wing specifically for that side of his business, and North Brink now saw a constant procession of carriages, as customers made their way to the house. He could not have chosen a more prestigious residence as a symbol of his success. By the age of forty he had become one of the most eminent citizens of Wisbech. His wife bore him four more children, yet out of the seven only one daughter and three sons reached maturity. Of those, only William, born in 1790, and Algernon, born in 1803, were to join their father in banking, helping to carry on the business after his death in 1833.

Jonathan Peckover was seventy-eight when he died, leaving a fortune to his widow and four surviving children. Bank House now had an excellent library, a collection of paintings and some magnificent gardens. It was a legacy that was, in the end, to benefit more than his immediate family.

Both William and Algernon continued to be true benefactors to the town, as their father had wished. Following on from his literary society, they founded the Wisbech Museum Society in 1835, serving respectively as President and Treasurer, arranging loan and endowment funds, putting in some of their own money for the construction of new premises in 1846 (which were, incidentally, officially opened in 1847 by none other than Sir Harry Smith, the Hero of Aliwal). They also helped to purchase nineteen acres of land to give Wisbech its first public park, and were active in local government for many years. Algernon was councillor from 1839 to 1847 and an alderman from 1847 to 1859. William was the Borough Treasurer until he died in 1877, when his brother Algernon succeeded him.

But that is still only part of the story. The Peckovers were equally interested in social welfare and health, giving generously to the founding of the North Cambridgeshire Hospital in 1873. In addition they gave their support to the Boys' Life Brigade, the Bible Society, the Wisbech Working Men's Club and, of course, the Quakers.

Algernon was also a gifted artist and architect who helped to design several of the properties on North Brink, including the new

Quaker Meeting House, and houses for the rest of his family. For a time it seems as if North Brink belonged to the dynasty of the Peckovers. Wisteria House, Harecroft House and Sibalds Holme were all the homes of various members of the Peckover family, and all were only a few yards from Bank House, where the widowed Mrs Jonathan Peckover still lived with her son William.

Out of four generations of such wise and philanthropic people it is unfair to single out the contribution of one more than another, but I think that Algernon has to receive a little more attention, mainly because his own eight children were to perpetuate the family's good works for a long time to come. His daughter, Priscilla Hannah, was particularly active in local affairs, with a gift for organization and leadership. She was also a linguist and translated Quaker tracts into many languages, worked all her life for the peace movement, and was an accomplished artist.

Algernon's sons, Alexander and Jonathan, were equally industrious in their efforts to improve life for the people of Wisbech. Jonathan died unmarried at the age of forty-six, but Alexander did marry and have three children before his wife Eliza died, aged thirty-one. His sister Priscilla then stepped in to bring up his very young family.

It was Alexander who took over Bank House when his uncle William died in 1877, and it was he who was to extend the library with his own collection of rare first editions and manuscripts, including all but one of the printed Greek Bibles and Testaments published before 1530. Writing about his library he said: 'My MSS speak for themselves. They are very valuable & several over 1,000 years old. There are several first editions of early recent writers: Milton's *Paradise Lost* & *Regained*, the latter the most difficult to meet with.'

In 1893 Alexander was nominated by Prime Minister William Gladstone to be the Lord Lieutenant of Cambridgeshire, to which Queen Victoria readily consented. In 1894 he received an honorary Doctorate of Law degree from Cambridge University, and in 1907 he was elevated to the peerage. He died in 1919 at the age of eighty-nine, by which time civilization had endured the tragedy of the First World War, which overshadowed many of the ideals in which he had believed.

His daughter, Alexandrina, is the last member of the family I will mention, for she was to be the last Peckover to live in Bank House, and it was she who arranged for the house to pass to the National

Trust when she died in 1948. It was only then that the premises
became known officially as Peckover House.

Can any family have made a worthier contribution to a local
community or, for that matter, to mankind as a whole? There are
dynasties and dynasties, benefactors and tyrants. No one can doubt
the generous spirit in which the Peckovers spent their wealth. I shall
await Christina Swaine's ambitious work with some eagerness. It
has all the makings of another *Forsyte Saga* and by then many more
people will be aware of the family's lasting achievements.

As I said earlier, I had really gone to Wisbech to find out more
about Peckover House before getting caught up in the history of the
family (and, I can assure you, I am more than grateful for the diver-
sion). Fortunately for me, Christina is also a Room Steward at the
house, and so I was able to enjoy a personally conducted tour of the
property and find out more about the National Trust's plans for its
jubilee in 1998. The house already attracts 10,000 visitors a year,
and I am sure this number will increase when the details of the celebration are announced.

The house is normally open on Wednesdays, Saturdays, Sundays
and Bank Holiday Mondays. I had arranged to meet Christina there
at two-thirty on a Wednesday, which also turned out to be the
hottest day of the year. There were already quite a few people looking round, so the house felt alive and lived-in rather than a
museum. From one of the inner rooms I could hear a piano being
played. I asked Christina if it was real or just recorded. It was real
and added a pleasant dimension to my journey into the past.

Room by room we went through the house, being reminded by
letters, drawings, paintings and furniture of the kind of life the
Peckovers would have known when they lived there. Because it was
so hot many of the windows were open, allowing a warm breeze to
permeate the house. Although the Peckovers were Quakers and
believed in a simple and unadorned life, they had been quite
prepared to accept many of the house's original eighteenth century
ornamentations and florid styles.

The room I was most anxious to see was the room which used to
be Alexander's library and which, as part of the jubilee celebrations,
is to be restored. Book-shelves are to be built into the extensive
recesses either side of the fireplace and restocked, as far as possible
with the kind of books that would have furnished a Victorian
library. Sadly, the original bookshelves were taken out years ago and
can never be replaced, but at least an effort is being made to recre-

ate the library in something like its former splendour. It was in that room that I was able to see the magnificent portrait of Alexander painted, when he was the Lord Lieutenant of Cambridgeshire, by his son-in-law James Doyle Penrose. He is shown wearing his Cambridge University Doctor of Law's gown and holding one of his precious early printed bibles.

But the portrait that appealed to me most was the one of his brother, Jonathan, who died at the age of forty-six. He had one of the kindest faces you could ever wish to see, with the most gentle eyes and an expression of goodness. I commented on this to Christina and had the immediate impression that he was her favourite too. What he might have achieved had he lived longer and married is hard to say but, in his relatively short life, he had done enough to show that he was a true Peckover. He founded the Wisbech Working Men's Club and Institute in 1864, enabling uneducated men to meet together to discuss a wide range of subjects and hear talks from local scholars. Jonathan himself gave a lecture on *The Heroes of the Fens* and encouraged the men to improve their reading so that they could be better informed. He was clearly a natural teacher who loved contact with ordinary people. He also started the First Day School (the Quakers' name for Sunday School) held at the Friend's Meeting House irrespective of the children's own religious backgrounds, if they had any. The Peckover families had always been made to look to Thomas Clarkson as an example of how to help others, and they, in their turn, were doing the same for the less privileged young people of the town. The children liked Jonathan because he had a sense of humour and appeared less severe than some members of the family.

When my tour of the house was complete we went into the large Victorian garden for some fresh air. Some children were playing croquet on one of the lawns, whilst their parents sat in the shade enjoying afternoon tea. Naturally the garden is full of unusual trees and plants. Grapes were ripening in the hot August sun, and herbaceous borders embroidered the paths with brilliant colours. Visitors wandered leisurely about, resting occasionally on one of the many seats placed in shady corners. Christina was taking me round to see a very secluded summer-house with little stained-glass windows, when we met the Property Manager and Head Gardener, Glyn Jones. He invited us into his own peaceful garden within the grounds to enjoy a long, cool drink of Ribena as he outlined some of the plans for the jubilee celebrations. He and his team of volunteer workers had some busy months ahead – lectures, concerts, banquets, garden parties and the refurbishing of the library.

When our walk round the garden resumed I stopped to look at a small graveyard, a crescent of little headstones, each one bearing the name of one of the Peckover's beloved cats. It seemed to sum up the family's reverence for all life and their implicit kindness. In fact cats are still a feature of the house and gardens. As we sat on one of the wrought-iron seats, looking across the now empty lawn, one of them came over to join us. He was called Medlar and was named after the medlar tree – though I gather he could just as easily have been called 'meddler', because he carried curiosity beyond what is normally expected of the feline race. There is another resident cat called Mulberry but that one is too shy to take much interest in visitors. Medlar was quite happy to make room for himself on our seat and purr his own contribution to the conversation.

We continued to talk about several members of the Peckover family, down to the last one to live in the house – Alexandrina, who had made it possible for us, and thousands of others, to enjoy a glimpse of their world. It was not difficult to imagine a few scenes from those times. The spacious gardens allowed their ghosts to drift over the lawns and along the paths. I thought of the portraits in the house and of some of the paintings by Algernon and Priscilla Hannah. I thought of Alexander and Jonathan, of the letters, books and furnishings that were part of their lives. It was not really so long ago, but how different life is now.

By the time we got back to the house the visitors had all gone, and the stewards had locked up until the next open day. It was almost six o'clock, with no hint that the temperature was going to drop a few degrees before darkness. The River Nene was now flowing brown and giddily out to sea, as if it too was anxious to cool down. The houses on the South Brink also gained from the early evening sunlight, which made them mellow and almost as dignified at their neighbours opposite. Beyond the bridge the monument to Thomas Clarkson stood out sharply against the sky, as if it had just been unveiled.

With the working day over and most of the offices and shops closed, the noise of traffic had lessened considerably. There was now a calm, more sedate atmosphere about the place. As I stood for a few moments reflecting on my interesting day I could not help but think again of the town's contribution to Fenland life, and beyond. What I also realized was that it did not end with the nineteenth century. Its citizens continue with the good work that was started then, in education, medicine, the arts, farming and industry. How many will have monuments erected in their honour I cannot say but, of this I am sure, many will be worth remembering.

ᴄᴏ 17 ᴏᴠ

A Night to Remember

It is not often that dreams come true exactly as we would wish. This is even more true when they are the dreams of a village that wants a special occasion to be a great success. But the people of Parson Drove must have slept well at the end of their first John Peck Festival weekend, knowing that everything they had hoped for had not only happened but surpassed their expectations.

The idea for the Festival was born some two or three years ago when a group of people became aware of the importance of the diary that farmer John Peck had kept for nearly forty years of his working life. I was fortunate to get involved in this discovery when I was writing my book *In Fen Country Heaven*. The Reverend John Seaman, then the vicar of Parson Drove, wrote to me about the diary, urging that something should be done to make Peck's account of his life in the Fens better known. Dian Blawer had already spent many hours working on the manuscripts of the diary, which were kept in the Wisbech and Fenland Museum, and there had been an exhibition about Peck's life and work which attracted much interest.

The question now being asked was, would it be possible to start a John Peck Society, with a view to eventually raising enough money to get at least a selection from the diary published? When John Seaman suggested that John Peck could become the Francis Kilvert of the Fens I became even more intrigued and gladly accepted his invitation to meet Dian Blawer and Bridget Holmes (a Peck relative) to discuss ways of making these intentions a reality. After looking through several of the diary entries I was immediately aware of their quality and agreed with the idea of organizing an inaugural festival, to be held in the village during a weekend nearest to John Peck's birthday, which was 21 August 1797.

In the meantime more work was done on the diary, and in August 1997, exactly two hundred years after his birth, the Wisbech and Fenland Museum published an excellent little book by Dian Blawer – *John Peck of Parson Drove: An Exceptional Fenman*. It was just what was needed to whet the appetite for more and to give the festival weekend an even sharper focus as the village celebrated the life of its most distinguished neighbour.

Enthusiasm is a great breeder of ideas, and the festival soon involved many of the Parson Drove people, as well as some from Wisbech, in its organization. The weekend would also be a Flower Festival, and it was decided that it should be held in the now redundant church of St John the Baptist, which was where the Peck family had worshipped. There could also be a concert there on the Saturday evening, followed by a buffet supper, and a Festival Evensong on the Sunday with a well-known guest preacher. It was clear that the committee was determined to make it a momentous occasion, and they worked extremely hard to make it so.

I had suggested that my good friend of many years, Ronald Blythe, should be invited as the main guest for the weekend, especially as he was the editor of the *Penguin Book of Diaries* and was about to publish his own account of a life in rural England: *Words from Wormingford*. He was delighted to be asked and readily agreed to come and stay with us for the weekend, so that he could be part of both the Saturday and Sunday celebrations.

August 1997 was, you may remember, a month of high temperatures and unbearable humidity. Everyone suffered some degree of lethargy as the sticky atmosphere continued day and night. The Saturday evening of the festival, 23 August, was as uncomfortably warm as any climate could be. When the church of St John the Baptist was in regular use it was renowned for being extremely cold, but no one who sat in the audience that night would have believed it. The church was packed to the doors, everyone in their lightest summer clothes and fanning themselves with programmes long before the concert started.

We had driven over to Parson Drove on some of the back roads, so that Ronald could enjoy that wonderful expanse of fen country between Crowland and Wisbech. The evening light was perfect. To our left the Lincolnshire Fens stretched for miles into the hazy distance; to our right the Cambridgeshire Fens doubled the expanse of space and sky. The water in the dykes glistened, and the reeds glowed like golden heraldry.

We parked our car in the yard of what used to be the last working woad mill, which was pulled down in 1914, and immediately met up with some friends from Wiltshire who had also become interested in John Peck. As we walked up the path to the church porch we could hear and feel the buzz of excitement from within.

The church had been transformed with its imaginative floral displays and exhibition of Peck memorabilia. I was particularly delighted to see that some of the ladies responsible for the flower arrangements had taken John Peck's interest in hot-air balloons as a theme for their creations – he would have liked that. Others had been inspired by his love of travel and fen drainage. And there, between the choir stalls, sat the village band waiting to entertain us. To the purist it might have seemed a little unbalanced, with five or six cornets, a euphonium and B-flat bass, but it was just right for the occasion.

The major part of the programme, rightly, was devoted to readings from the diary. Ronald Blythe and I batted first, our words running nervously between wickets as we read short extracts alternately, he from the pulpit, I from the lectern. The script, which had been compiled by Dian Blawer, created a vivid portrait of village life as seen through the eyes of this local farmer, who also had a considerable talent as a writer:

What a fine thing is a village Fair! To see the happy smiling faces of the throng assembled is truly delightful. And then the preparations – the sweeping, washing and scouring up, the white lead and whiting, and the green doors and brown shutters fresh-varnished. The new frocks and jackets for the children, the new caps and ribbons for those of larger growth. The gingerbread and nuts tempting the poor boy, rich with his two pence saved for the occasion. The merry fiddle, not playing tunes but something like them to dancers that never went to dancing school. The walking arm-in-arm of many a happy couple, perhaps their first meeting, who are afterwards to become partners for life. Friendly visits of uncles, aunts and cousins, and an old man's tale of when he was a boy, all mix up and make a village fair a scene of delight.

John Peck wrote that on 24 June 1831 and I wonder if the scene could have been better described by Francis Kilvert, or even Charles Dickens! There were equally fine descriptions of some of the great storms that swept across the Fens in the nineteenth century;

accounts of Peck's involvement in the improvement of drainage in the Fens; of the agricultural depression that ruined many farmers and caused ugly unrest among the farm-workers, who sometimes took the law into their own hands. There were lovely vignettes of family life and an amusing recollection of a trip to Paris where, among other things, John and his friend ate snail pâté (which they did not know about until they saw the shells in the hotel yard the following morning – but, as he said, 'it was too late to be sick!').

These readings were shared by people from the village, by members of the family – including Nigel Peck, a direct descendant, who had flown over from Australia especially to be part of these celebrations. We also had some vocal interludes by a couple calling themselves simply The Caseys, and a selection of popular pieces from the band. The last reading, appropriately, was given by Dian Blawer, whose moving and sensitive account of John Peck's final days and death, left many people in the audience unable to hold back the tears, not only of sorrow but also of gratitude for a great man for whom, as Dian said, the whole village was now a memorial – a living memorial. At that moment we all forgot how hot we were. The privilege of being there outweighed any discomfort. And then, as an impromptu gesture to the visitors from down under, the band brought the concert to an end by playing *Waltzing Matilda*.

It will give you some idea of how devoted and conscientious the committee members were when I tell you that some of them slept in the church overnight to protect the priceless exhibition and flower displays. Two friends of ours, who came to this country from Vienna many years ago, still saw it as a quintessentially English custom. I'm sure that Jack won't mind my quoting him: 'It was so English it wasn't true. There was the bossy woman telling me to move my car; there was the lady who was so embarrassed when I asked for the toilets; and then that brass band! And the display was quite impressive . . . . Long may it continue.'

We drove home through the balmy late-night air, across the Fens now sleeping in the warm dark. In the distance we could see the floodlit image of Crowland Abbey and the distant lights of a city that had no idea of the fun we'd had at Parson Drove.

Next day, making sure that Ronnie had his Address prepared for the Sunday afternoon Evensong, I agreed to take him on a brief tour of the Fens, including the Holme Fen Posts, the site of Whittlesea Mere, then Whittlesey St Mary's church with its noble spire, Thorney Abbey, Crowland Abbey (in daylight) and a few views in between that I thought would give our guest an even deeper insight into a landscape that had produced such an important part of this country's history. Although the temperature was still very warm we had spells of light rain, and the low, grey clouds made the stubble in the harvest fields look bright amber. Ronnie had long wanted to visit Crowland Abbey, and I was pleased that he was not disappointed. The humid drizzle added something extra to the impact of its strange beauty and antiquity. We walked through the ruined, roofless nave, stepped slowly under the slender dog-tooth arch towards the burial ground where once the choir stood. One ornately carved headstone had been pushed over on to its back by vandals and had gathered into its recesses pools of rainwater and leaves reflecting the sky. It was as if the stone had become its own stained-glass window, with the eroded inscription like engraved letters relying now on the light from above.

After a quick lunch we were on our way back to Parson Drove for the Festival Evensong, which coincided with the Feast Day of St Bartholomew the Apostle. There was a very good congregation, and the service was conducted with impressive dignity by the rural dean of Wisbech, the Reverend Robert Bull. Ronald's address focused on the importance of genealogy from the Hebrews to the present day and the relevance of a family tree in preserving the history of a family, such as the Pecks.

At the end of the service I was talking to a man who I think is undoubtedly in the John Peck mould – Alwyn Johnson, farmer, churchwarden, musician, local historian and guardian of his village. Referring to the success of the weekend, and especially the Saturday evening concert, he said, 'I've never seen anything like it in all my life. It was marvellous. A night to remember. I'm very, very happy.' (I could see from his shining eyes that he meant every word.) He, and the rest of the people involved in this special event, have every right to be pleased with what they achieved. We had all spent the weekend celebrating the life of one man, but I believe we were also celebrating the life of a village community that has contributed much to the long traditions and riches of the Fens. I can think of many who would like to have been part of that experience.

Whether a John Peck Society will be established out of this inaugural festival or not it is difficult to say. I am certain that Parson Drove will want to organize a similar event next year to keep the interest alive, and I hope I shall be invited to be part of it. If one dream can come true, so, surely, can others. I, for one, believe that this lovely church ought to be brought back to life more often. John Peck might have achieved more than he imagined.

I know that Ronald Blythe was tremendously impressed with all that the people had done. He wrote to me a couple of days later, 'I was so touched by the toil which had gone into the Festival and at seeing yet again how the women of a country parish reinstate the glories of this ancient shrine. That church is too splendid to be redundant . . . . . The Parson Drovians must miss it so. And wasn't the Rural Dean excellent? Those serious pauses – so telling.'

Because it had all been so overwhelming I felt I had to go back on the Tuesday of the following week to make sure that it had not all been part of some fantasy. The church was still there, and the tree which had been planted in memory of John Peck, and some flowers in the porch, but there were now only echoes of the jubilation which had so recently brought it to life. It was as if the church had gone back to sleep, undisturbed even by any ghosts that had been woken with it for its brief rejoicing.

P.S. I am delighted to report that The John Peck Society is now in existence with an initial membership of fifty and more to come.

ᴄᴏ 18 ᴏᴄ
Birthrooms and Destinies

I wonder what your feelings are when you stand in the room where a famous person was born. On the very few occasions when I have had that experience I have, so I convinced myself, felt almost on holy ground, where even a whispered comment seemed inappropriate and a raised voice would have been sacrilegious.

Now, you may think that such an over-reverent attitude smacks of idolatry, but if you have stood in any of those simple rooms where Mozart, Beethoven, Shakespeare or Thomas Hardy were born, you will know what I mean. There is a presence that somehow makes you aware of the life that began there and then went on to enrich the world.

I had the same feeling a few days ago standing in the small room of a large house in Wisbech where, on 3 December 1838, a baby girl was born who was to earn immortality in two different ways – by improving the quality of life for millions of under privileged people and by helping to make the most beautiful parts of this country available to other generations for all time. Her name was Octavia Hill, one of the daughters of James Hill's third marriage and very much a child of her unusual parents.

The strikingly impressive house on South Brink is still there, almost opposite the more famous buildings associated with the Peckover family that I have already written to you about. There is a small blue plaque on the wall which is a masterpiece of under-statement.

OCTAVIA HILL
One of the Founders of the National Trust
was born here 1838.

144

That inscription covers but a brief chapter in her life-story, and it only came about because of her other, more important, work which culminated in the Octavia Hill Housing Trust, with 1,300 houses in London alone. Her original ideas and vision were to influence the development of inner-city communities for a hundred years, and still do. Her methods were practical and authoritative, her philosophy straightforward and humanitarian. Her aim was simply to make 'lives noble, homes happy, and family life good'.

This was not an entirely uncommon ambition among many comfortably-off young Victorian ladies who were aware of the appalling misery of the poor people crowded into our cities. But Octavia's desire to do something about it went beyond well-meaning pity. She knew how to put her theories into practice because she had grown up in a family of free-thinking, determined individuals who took matters into their own hands, sometimes impulsively, even disastrously, but always with courage. How else do you get things done if you are not prepared to take risks, to withstand criticism and put your reputation at stake? Caution can repress too much, and the Hill family nearly always went for broke. They won, and they lost.

Octavia Hill may have learned much from her father but she also received a lasting inspiration from her maternal grandfather, Dr Thomas Southwood Smith, who was a powerful influence in those days of social reform. It was through him that Octavia was to know Robert Owen and later John Ruskin, two important men in her life who each deserve a letter to themselves – but I must not digress more than is necessary.

I have said in a previous Letter that several people are often needed to make the success of one person possible, and I can only write to you about all these staggering achievements because others have been kind enough to involve me in their story. So I had better tell you how I became enthusiastic about the Hills before giving you the impression that I am an authority on the subject.

Once again I am indebted to the town of Wisbech and have to say again that the value of a place, village, town or country will always depend on the quality of the individuals who belong to it and help to shape its image. A place is only as good as its people, and if Wisbech has featured largely in these Letters it is because its citizens, both past and present, have made it what it is. In turn, the place also helps to make the people, which is something that

Octavia Hill believed, but that is another debate we must return to at some other time.

I knew very little of this remarkable lady until I met one of her most devoted disciples, Peter Clayton at the Octavia Hill Birthplace Museum on the South Brink. I realized immediately that I was in the presence of a man with a mission – a mission which began some years ago whilst he was researching the history of London, a subject which he also knows very well (after all, it's the city where he spends part of his working week). One can smell enthusiasm a mile off, and he has it. Although in charge of, and responsible for, the imaginative presentation of the museum's several rooms, he is the first to insist that he has only been able to get this far because of a team of equally dedicated volunteer helpers and support from other organizations. Nevertheless, someone has to have the idea, patience, energy and determination to get things done – rather like Octavia herself – so Peter was the man I went to see. He had three or four other duties to perform at the same time, but he is one of those lucky people who can layer his thinking and give each task the attention it requires.

It was soon clear to me that to appreciate the achievements of Octavia Hill one needed to know quite a bit about the family that produced her, for she was very much a child of her parents, who between them not only shaped her personality and beliefs but also allowed her to learn from their mistakes and experience.

I became especially interested in her father, James Hill, who was the son of a then well-known Peterborough family of merchants trading in malt, hops, maize, barley, coal, timber and spirits and which was involved in banking and running a small fleet of packet boats which operated on the River Nene between Peterborough and Wisbech, a distance of twenty-one miles.

In 1818 James Hill decided to leave the city for Wisbech and try his luck at running his own business, an adventure which led to his falling in love. His wife-to-be was Ann Jecks, the daughter of a wealthy merchant who lived on North Brink, not far from the Peckovers. Although Ann was to bear him four children, she was not a strong person and died in 1832. By this time James had already suffered his first business failure, which was to undermine his confidence. In 1825 his bank was unable to honour its obligations and, along with more than a hundred small provincial banks in the country at that time, went under. James Hill, entrepreneur, merchant and local banker was bankrupt. He was now almost friendless, largely through his own uncompromising and outspoken attitude towards others. He was one man who certainly did not fit easily into Wisbech society, governed as it was by the church and the Quakers – alias the Peckovers. Hill was a radical, a Unitarian, an advocate of secular education and a champion of the poor. He attacked both Church and Chapel, the aristocracy and privileged classes, made public his belief in Free Trade and freedom of speech, and supported the social reformer Robert Owen, who wanted to create a new society of co-operative living. In 1837 he involved himself in the Parliamentary election in Peterborough, believing that his family's reputation in that city would help to attract votes. It didn't. But James was nothing if not a survivor. In 1832 he had married his dead wife's sister and was now determined to make a name for himself in journalism. Yet with each new hope of triumph, with each glimmer of success, he seemed destined to face yet another disaster. His second wife died, leaving him a widower again, now with six children to care for. That was one task he could not tackle alone.

Attracted by the writings of Caroline Southwood Smith on the subject of education, he wrote to her asking if she would consider becoming a governess to his family. He must himself have been a very persuasive man with the pen, for not only did she accept that appointment in 1835 she also agreed to marry him and was to bear him three more daughters, including Octavia in 1838.

By 1836 he felt that life was offering him another new start, and he began publishing his radical newspaper *Star in the East*, in which the philosophy of Robert Owen's new society was expounded, praised and proclaimed as the only true and fair life. Its aim was 'to help forward the cause of humanity'. To further this cause Robert Owen was invited to Wisbech in 1838 to address an audience made up not only of sympathizers but of cynics and those vehemently opposed to such a co-operative system of equality in work and possession. Owen also lectured in March and Peterborough and saw a definite need for the establishment of a colony in the Fens similar to the one he had founded at New Lanark. This idea met with some initial success, but it takes a long time to change human nature, if one ever can.

Perhaps you will allow me to delay the progress of Octavia's story yet again by telling you something about her mother. You will, I'm sure, see that it is all relative and helps to explain how such a mixture of genes, talents, backgrounds and opportunities were all to manifest themselves in the remarkable child the new Mrs Hill produced.

Caroline's father, Dr Thomas Southwood Smith, was born in Somerset in 1788 and brought up in a family of strict Calvinists, but when he became a student at the Bristol Baptist College, he soon found himself disillusioned with such a harsh creed, which allowed little room for love or forgiveness. By the age of twenty he decided that he could no longer support any religion that ignored the poor and, worse still, condemned them to the wrath of God for actions which were a direct result of the squalid living conditions imposed on them by a selfish society. He was soon preaching what Octavia Hill, his granddaughter, was later to proclaim as her beliefs:

> It is not by sweeping general measures, it is not by widespread changes, it is not by legal enactments, but face to face and heart to heart, that pauperism must be dealt with . . . it is the friendly help that takes the degradation out of it.

Like her grandfather, Octavia knew that poverty was at the root of most social evils and that a sanctimonious condemnation of poor people forced to live in slums was a betrayal of the true Christian faith. Perhaps I should say here that she was to turn from her father's Unitarian beliefs and become a regular worshipper in the Church of England.

But back to Thomas Southwood Smith, who as a qualified doctor was to work for many years as a physician to the London Fever Hospital and devote most of his life to the improvement of living conditions for those he saw condemned to such an appalling environment. He was a public health reformer and a socialist, fighting against child labour and the exploitation of women who were made to do the work of pit-ponies in the nation's coal-mines. And that was only just over 150 years ago!

It is not surprising that his daughter Caroline should one day appeal to James Hill and be ready to join him in his campaigns to bring about some equality, both in Wisbech and later in London. They were to become followers of Robert Owen and a daunting couple to face. In July 1837 they opened in Wisbech a school which was housed in a small purpose-built Greek-style building as a temple to education. Caroline had already written of her support for the Pestalozzi method of teaching – or perhaps I should say *learning* – and now had the chance to put it to the test. Writing in her husband's paper *Star in the East* she said:

> the tender minds of infants can only receive a certain quantity; we take so much pains to cram them with errors that nature's beautiful activity is checked. The infant becomes the passive recipient of false impressions and the man becomes an imperfect being.

The children at the Hills' school of enlightenment were consequently allowed a great deal of freedom to explore and to develop at their own pace. Curiosity was fostered, the search for truth encouraged rather than imposed. No religion was taught. Kindness, justice and understanding were the only acceptable creed. It is little wonder that this establishment soon became known locally as The Infidel School.

These experiments in education, together with James Hill's radical views and abruptness, soon made him a social outcast, at least to some. The poorer people of the town naturally saw him as something of a saviour, especially when he opened his school in the evenings as a Hall of the People and offered them free education. It was one of these parents, a William Hodson, who was to help in establishing the Owenite colony near Manea, which I hope to come back to at a later date.

I hope I have already said enough to show you how all these strong-minded people came together and why we have such an incredible story in the first place. Without the background and parentages concerned there would have been no story about Octavia to tell.

Despite all the family's setbacks her own parents were devoted to each other in a common cause that was simply an extension of their ability to love. Caroline was to write of her husband after his death

> He drew upon himself much hatred by his struggle against abuses, but he did not struggle in vain. . . . A man of large, and liberal, and friendly kindly spirit, who would not willingly have done harm to anybody, but, on the contrary, would have done good to all.

He was a man of immense energy and talent, who was, in his wife's words, 'almost superhuman'. Yet, despite that, and because of many circumstances beyond his control, James Hill went bankrupt again in 1840. All his assets were sold, and the family left Wisbech to start their next adventure.

By the time I had spent three hours with the superhuman enthusiasm of Peter Clayton I was exhausted and felt it was time to leave Wisbech too, though far from bankrupt. I had amassed a wealth of information and needed time to myself to analyse my impressions, as well as all the history.

In fact it might be a good idea to break off the narrative right here, so that I can start my next Letter to you with a greater determination to concentrate on Octavia Hill and her legacy to mankind. I can assure you that the rest of the story is worth waiting for, and she will have centre stage. The one thing you must be wanting to know by now is what she was like as a person, physically as well as intellectually, so perhaps I ought to give you an appetiser. Not only do we have portraits of her, but fortunately several of her friends left excellent and often frank descriptions of her. Although she had a becoming beauty, she seldom bothered to make herself look

Octavia Hill (*c.* 1900)

attractive. As her life-long friend Henrietta Rowland Barnett said of her, 'she did not dress, she only wore clothes', and in a photograph of her taken round about 1900, when she would have been sixty-two, one could easily imagine her as a Mother Superior in the Sisters of Serenity.

Yet what determination there was beneath that calm exterior. And what a very different world she chose to work in, instead of a convent. She was struggling in a London not all that far removed from the soot-covered, over-crowded and brutal city described so vividly by William Blake:

> I wander thro' each charter'd street
> Near where the charter'd Thames does flow,
> And mark in every face I meet
> Marks of weakness, marks of woe.
>
> In every cry of every Man,
> In every infant's cry of fear,
> In every voice, in every ban,
> The mind-forged manacles I hear.
>
> How the chimney-sweeper's cry
> Every blackening Church appals,
> And the hapless soldier's sigh
> Runs in blood down palace walls;
>
> But most thro' midnight streets I hear
> How the youthful harlot's curse
> Blasts the new-born infant's tear
> And blights with plagues the marriage hearse.

Children as young as five and six were still being sold for £8 to work as chimney-sweeps and made to climb up inside the black chimneys still hot from fires that had only just gone out. It was never an easy or comfortable city for anyone with a social conscience, and Octavia Hill must have shared Blake's anger and despair more than once.

Perhaps she also shared his hope, and would have said with him:

> I will not cease from mental fight,
> Nor shall my sword sleep in my hand,
> Till we have built Jerusalem
> In England's green & pleasant land.

As I think my next Letter will prove, she went a long way towards achieving that.

∞ 19 ∞

Bringing Colour to the Colourless

O ctavia Hill was only two years old when the family left Wisbech, and you might think her connections with the Fens should end there. Not so. What followed that move to London is so significant that the Birthplace Museum in Wisbech is fully justified in its efforts to make her tremendous contribution to humanity better known, not only in the Fens from which she came but throughout the rest of the land. Only yesterday I spoke to a well-read and well-informed man who knew of her simply as one of the founders of the National Trust. He had no idea of the scale of her work in housing reform.

When her family left Wisbech in 1848 they did not leave all their troubles behind them. Her father was now exhausted and depressed, so much so that Caroline was to record in her memoirs that he had a 'temporary fit of insanity'. The strain on the marriage and the children was too much. James and Caroline decided to separate, and, although she still admired him for what he had achieved, she became the dominant influence on her daughters' lives.

She and the girls now lived in Finchley, north London, which was still rural in those days, and the children were free to play in the fields, climb trees, jump ditches and enjoy all the adventures of children's invented games without fear of coming to any harm. In 1851, however, Caroline decided to move into London itself, so that she could extend her social and educational reforms closer to the problems. One of her aims was to get women accepted in several areas of employment and to be suitably recompensed for their labours. Writing in *The Illustrated London News* (which was started by a Lincolnshire man, Herbert Ingram of Boston) she argued that:

the whole burden of the main influence of society need not necessarily rest, as now, on men ... there are many women who would be
glad to meet with remunerative occupation.

Caroline now had the support of men like Robert Owen, William
Wilberforce and, eventually, John Ruskin, all of whom were to
influence Octavia's own ideas when she began her work.

At the age of fourteen Octavia was put in charge of the Ragged
School children, where the girls made toys and received a very basic
education. When she took over she was appalled at the strict disci-
pline and the intimidating lists of rules and punishments that hung
on the walls, so she tore them down. She believed that she would
get the girls to work better for her through mutual trust, respect
and co-operation. Workers, she maintained, were individuals and
had to be treated as such. This was considered an eccentric notion
in the middle of the nineteenth century, but she persevered.

Living now in the centre of London, she saw the scale of poverty
and misery around her. From her own home, a cold and gloomy
house in an ugly street, she looked out of her window and wept for
those homeless people trudging through the rain and fog with their
haggard faces and bent backs.

Some years later she was to write an article entitled 'Colour,
Space and Music for the People' in the journal *The Nineteenth
Century*. In it she said:

> Till you can stay a little within the colourless, forlorn desolation of
> the houses in the worst courts, till you have lived among the monot-
> onous, dirty tints of the poor districts of London, you little know
> what the colours of your curtains, carpets, and wallpaper are to you.

Better housing for the poor became a priority in her campaign to
improve the quality of their lives. She also believed that the houses
themselves should be in better areas, with space around them, with
trees, parks and flowers. Octavia Hill was the originator of 'the
Green Belt' as early as 1888 – a fact which even the Oxford
Dictionary had to amend when it was pointed out. All people, she
claimed, were entitled to 'the healthy gift of air and joy, of plants
and flowers'. She was convinced that a place made the people, that
if the natural and social environments were right, if education and
the arts were freely available to people who were then living in

slums, better human beings would evolve as a result. It would take time, but it could be made to work.

What angered her as much as anything was the knowledge that there were plenty of empty houses in London, but the landlords would not rent them to undesirable tenants. (She asked one of their agents, 'But where *are* the poor to live?' and he replied, 'I don't know, but they must keep off the St John's Wood estate'.) There was only one answer. She must become a landlord herself, responsible for her own houses and tenants. To do this she turned to her friend John Ruskin, with whom she had been having art lessons. He advanced the money at five per cent interest, and in 1864 Octavia was able to purchase the first three properties, three-storied terraced houses in Paradise Place, off Marylebone. They were in an appalling state. In one house only eight panes of glass out of 192 were still intact; as many as nine people were living in one room, and most of the banisters had been broken down for firewood. The neighbourhood was then a notorious slum area which attracted crime and prostitution, but Octavia personally managed the houses and regularly collected the rents.

She was still only twenty-six, a quiet, stubborn and fearless young woman urged on by the need for reform. Slowly, and with some opposition, she began to educate her tenants in the running of their homes. This was no easy task, for the men did not want their womenfolk liberated by this self-righteous spinster. Their wives should be kept in their place, bearing children, providing meals and just being there when needed. But Octavia's restored faith in Christianity made her realize that faith and action went hand in hand, and she was even more determined to demonstrate that this was best expressed not in pious ritual but in compassion, hard work and humility. She now accepted that she needed the Church to renew her spiritual energies, but her beliefs could best be expressed in practical ways.

Paradise Place was a success, and this inspired her to buy other properties in areas where houses needed improving. Again John Ruskin came to her aid, and in 1866 five houses were bought in Freshwater Place. She also managed to get a small area cleared and planted with a garden and trees. She had always loved space; when she was a child she longed for a field so large that she could run in it forever. Had she spent more of her childhood in Wisbech than she did, I would be tempted to say that the Fens were responsible for this need, this passion for space. Perhaps in some ways they

were, for often in London she would say 'I feel that quiet beauty
and space would be more powerful to calm the wild excesses about
me than all my frantic striving'.

I do not think that 'frantic' is a word I would ever use about
Octavia Hill, and it is little wonder that her deep love of nature and
all its solitudes inspired in her the concept of the National Trust. It
is not only the recluse or creative artist who needs silence. Very
often the man or woman of action has to be alone to recharge the
batteries. I am often reminded of the wise words of Henry David
Thoreau, who wrote in his Journal on 7 January 1857:

> I come out to these solitudes where the problem of existence is
> simplified. I get a mile or two from the town into the stillness and
> solitude of nature.

Surely, that is what Octavia Hill felt, and I am sure she would have
responded with a grateful heart to the writings of the American
philosopher and naturalist.

In 1874 she was introduced to Canon Hardwick Rawnsley and
joined him in his campaign to stop the exploitation of the Lake
District for water supplies to Manchester and Lancashire. Together
they co-opted the legal brain of the solicitor Robert Hunter of the
Commons, Open Spaces, and Footpaths Preservation Society, which
had been set up in 1865, and launched their campaign to establish
a benevolent rather than commercial organization which would
work for the 'preservation of natural beauty and buildings of
historic interest' for the people. It took time, as all good ideas do,
but in 1895 the National Trust came into being and, as a result, now
owns over half a million acres of land, some 320 properties, and is
still growing. It is one of the great institutions of modern times, and
we owe an enormous debt to its founders.

It is appropriate that one of those properties to which we are
now allowed access, thanks to the National Trust, should be
Peckover House, about which I have already written. Another area
in the Fens which has been preserved is Wicken Fen, a place where
the problems of existence are simplified because one can find the
stillness and solitude of nature. Is it too much to hope that the
birthplace of Octavia Hill should also be protected in the same way,
for all time?

Octavia's own career continued to develop to almost superhuman proportions. She took on more houses, established more train-

ing courses for women, and became an active member of several committees responsible for safeguarding the parklands of London. She was also appointed by the Ecclesiastical Commissioners as manager of their properties in Southwark. During all this time she pursued her work in furthering education for adults as well as children.

One important fact to remember in this story is that Octavia Hill was a great believer in self-help, self-motivation and personal independence. She did not approve of hand-outs or even dole money. People should work for what they acquired. She disapproved of thoughtless charity dispensed by do-gooders with no concept of the real problem and she had little time for people who eased their consciences by just giving money in the hope that the problem would go away. She wanted those she helped to gain self-respect, to be proud of their work and not to sponge on society. She was always a practical woman more than a mere theorist. An idea had to work, just as people had to work, if a dream was worth pursuing.

Needless to say not everyone agreed with these principles. Fierce arguments interrupted the progress of Octavia Hill's plans, but she remembered her father and grandfather and stubbornly went on with what she believed to be best. She was not arrogant or aggressive, and she relied on persistent persuasion to win the day, which it usually did.

From John Singer Sargent's painting of her, which is in the National Portrait Gallery, we can see that he caught in her expression those combined qualities of kindness, determination, strength, vulnerability, radiance and reserve that both bemused and appealed to all those who knew her. As I said in my last Letter, we also have descriptions of her by her friends, especially Henrietta Rowland Barnett, who in her biography of her husband Canon Barnett recalled Octavia as an attractive woman who had 'soft and abundant hair and regular features, but the beauty of her face lay in her brown and very luminous eyes'. We also learn that she had a deep voice, which was seldom raised. She could win respect as much by a raised eyebrow as a firm command.

Comparing the portrait with the photograph I mentioned in my last Letter we can see that the camera captured a hint of her weariness, as well as contentment. Much had been achieved, but there was still much to be done. She did not see herself as a philanthropist or reformer wanting recognition, nor did she see herself as an idealist leaving others to do the work. She saw herself mainly as a teacher, someone instructing others in practical ways of improvement, so that their lives might be lived more abundantly, free from poverty and want.

Although she did not worry about physical beauty in herself, she was to strive for beauty in everything else: in places, in people, in art and worship. Her influence on society to this day is quite immeasurable. Her methods were copied in Holland, Germany, Russia and particularly in America, where the Octavia Hill Association of Philadelphia celebrated its centenary in 1996. Many local authorities and planning committees are only just catching up with her vision.

It has been fashionable to criticize the Victorians for most of the evils of the nineteenth century, and we cannot ignore the hypocrisy and double standards that existed then; but when you stop to consider some of the great personalities and liberators, the fearless campaigners and prophets of that revolutionary age, it is difficult to see how the twentieth century is going to surpass it on the credit side. It would be instructive to sit down and make a list of all the people living then who have made the world a better place now, in social welfare, industry, literature, music, education and public services, from libraries to lavatories and from art galleries to health clinics.

These two Letters have done far less than justice to the achievements of the Hill family and all their friends. I urge you to visit the Birthplace Museum in Wisbech and find out more from Peter Clayton and his colleagues. The opening times are the same as those for Peckover House.

When I left Peter that morning he was busy with a builder who had the task of converting the basement into an example of the typical single-room accommodation of the kind of house Octavia Hill worked so hard to transform, if not abolish; it is good for us to be reminded of how things have changed. By the time you read this Letter that project will have been completed, but the museum still has much work to do and will need financial and practical support for years to come. I came away tremendously uplifted and challenged by what I had learnt.

You can now understand why I said at the beginning of my previous Letter that the plaque on the wall of the house where Octavia was born is 'a masterpiece of understatement'. You would need a wall ten miles long to record the life of this remarkable woman who first drew breath in that small room on South Brink, Wisbech, on 3 December 1838 – the same year that the London-to-Birmingham railway line was opened and Charles Dickens published *Nicholas Nickleby*.

By the time Octavia died in 1912 the first decade of the new century had already seen many changes. Queen Victoria had died in 1901; finger-printing was introduced to combat crime; suffragettes were being sent to prison for trying to secure the vote for women; a National Old Age Pension was available for people over seventy; stars of the music hall were invited to take part in a Royal Command variety performance; radio had been invented; Great Britain now ruled one-fifth of the world; and the First World War was just two years away.

⤙ 20 ⤚

The Train Now Standing at Platform Two ...

As you know, we live not all that far from the Nene Valley
Railway. We can't see the trains but we can hear them, and it
takes no more than the whistle of a steam-engine owl-hooting its
way through the autumn afternoon for the imagination to be lured
away to some destination where we believe contentment will
remain untroubled by the demands of convention. Those two deep,
reedy notes can unlock memories of a forgotten world.

Our response, of course, will depend to some extent on our ages
and whether we had the kind of childhood in which steam was still
a great source of wonder and power. For some that haunting call
will be most evocative at night. For others it will have a greater
poignancy in winter, when the world is silenced by snow, and the
train slides slowly, like mercury, down the barometer of the darkening landscape.

My most memorable train journey at night will always be the one
taken with my wife one cold February from St Petersburg to
Moscow. That vast landscape was covered in snow, and the dense
birch forests crouched like frozen shadows on the mysterious plains
that I had previously only imagined from reading the great Russian
novelists. To our surprise the train was warm and comfortable. It
would have been quite easy to sleep, but why waste more than half
of the journey sleeping? This was probably going to be our only
chance of such an experience. So we stayed awake, peering out into
the dark and dying winter until we saw the first pink glimmer of
morning light breaking over the rooftops of Moscow.

Wherever, or whenever, one hears those rising and falling notes
of a train's whistle, they are much more than just a sound made by
the engine-driver obeying some regulation as he passes a certain

point on the track. They call us back to an age when boarding a train was an adventure. In my childhood we would not have been going to anywhere more exciting than Hunstanton or Skegness, but we might have been on the Orient Express or the Canadian Pacific, so great was our excitement. When I hear the Nene Valley engines now I can't help being reminded of a sentence in *Remembrance of Things Past*, where Proust describes the sound of a whistle 'punctuating the distance like the note of a bird in a forest' and imagines the 'deserted countryside through which a traveller is hurrying towards the nearby station'.

Trains at night do have a special appeal. The other evening I had to give a talk in Warboys, and, driving across the Fens, I'd almost forgotten how black and lonely they can feel at this time of the year. Familiar roads suddenly have a strangeness about them, as if they had never been travelled on before. Even though you know a road to be straight, you anticipate a bend. Landmarks, so clear in daylight, become invisible. Distant lights of villages tease before becoming reality.

But let me get back to the Nene Valley Railway. The length of its track is only seven-and-a-half miles long so its engines do not have much chance of gathering the speed to hurry towards the next station, yet those low, plaintive notes of the engine's whistle can still lure the mind back into remembered journeys of incredible length and romantic associations. For me the memories will inevitably be of summer holidays sixty years ago. The smell of engines is replaced by the smell of the sea and the salty taste of cockles and shrimps. Through the engine's smoke I begin to see the Punch and Judy show or the donkeys on the beach. And then I am touching again the slimy bladderwrack, squeezing the dark green blisters of each frond, and I automatically smell my fingers to see if the sensation is real.

Our friend, Stephen Brueton, who lives in the West Midlands, has had a passion for steam trains all his life. He can remember coming over as a boy from Birmingham to Peterborough just to gaze in wonder at some of the great engines on their way from King's Cross to the north of England and Scotland. He visits us two or three times a year and usually stays for a meal. When he hears the whistles echoing across the fields between our house and the river we can be sure that he will entertain us with a few more memories of those days when he collected the names and numbers of engines that are now part of railway history.

The only problem is that, despite several attempts to see one of the N.V.R. trains in action, he has so far been unlucky. Consequently, when he sits in our house and hears only the whistle he is convinced that there are no real trains at all, that the familiar notes are no more than an amplified tape-recording relayed over trees and rooftops to deceive our guests. One of these days, when we all have the time, we are determined to prove to him that it is no illusion. The trains do exist. The railway does have a timetable, plus train-drivers, ticket-collectors, a station, booking hall, refreshment room and passengers. At weekends, bank holidays and in peak seasons there are several trains a day, and at Christmas there is a Santa Special. If he wished, Stephen could even take a trip on Thomas the Tank Engine. Some trains can also be hired for wedding receptions, birthday parties and banquets – meals on wheels with a difference!

It is possible that he, and you, have actually seen one of the N.V.R. trains without knowing it for they have so far featured in more than a hundred films, documentaries and television productions, including *Secret Army*, *Love in a Cold Climate*, *East of the Moon*, *Dirty Dozen*, *Gaudy Night*, *Goldeneye*, *Middlemarch* and the early James Bond film *Octopussy* (which I recently watched on television, as I had never before seen a Bond movie).

The full history of the Nene Valley Railway goes back to 1845 and the birth of the railway industry as we know it today. For the purpose of this letter, though, I am only concerned with the society as it exists now, and I would like to tell you a little more about it.

The N.V.R. was established in 1977, but its original concept belongs to an earlier decade and, like many another flourishing enterprise, owes its existence to the dream of one man: the Reverend Richard Paten. Richard was an engineer who became a clergyman. As well as his love of steam he will also be remembered for his compassionate ministry, his community work in a growing multiracial city, and his disarming modesty; although the son of a prosperous and well-known family of wine-merchants and hoteliers, Richard decided on a very different vocation. I have known him for many years and have enjoyed conversations with him on local history, literature and art. We were friends of the artist John Hutton, who was one of the most colourful characters in Peterborough during the 1950s and 1960s. (Richard's mother was also a pupil at Miss Gibson's private school for girls in the Cathedral precincts – where, you will remember, Edith Cavell was once a student-teacher.)

It was after a visit to North America that Richard had the idea for preserving something of this country's long railway traditions. Nationalization, modernization and Dr Beeching had somehow knocked the romance out of trains. Faced with a characterless diesel, engine-drivers felt a bit like the old ploughmen forced to give up their horses, who used to say 'there's no fun in patting a tractor'. To the old railwaymen steam engines must have been living creatures that really breathed, panted, had fire in their bellies and blew whistles. Richard Paten was certainly not prepared to let the steam engine become the dinosaur of railway history. In 1968 he bought one of the last steam locomotives owned by British Rail, with the original intention of exhibiting it on a plinth outside the city's Regional College. But the engine was in such good condition that it was decided that, far from becoming a museum piece, it should be restored for active service. Steam trains were not prehistoric, they were living legends.

I am old enough to remember when Peterborough had two railway stations – the North, and the East, serving the separate needs and regions of the country. Richard's purchase, 73050, was to be found a new home at the now redundant East station and, on 28 March 1969, the Peterborough branch of the East Anglia Locomotive Preservation Society came into being with sixteen members. A year later the interest had grown sufficiently for the branch to become a tree in its own right, and so the Peterborough Locomotive Society was born, with a very clear view of what it wanted to do.

By this time the formerly modest city of Peterborough was undergoing its own transition with an expansion into Greater Peterborough. The newly created Development Corporation had plans to double the population within fifteen years, and maybe more beyond that. This can usually be good news for a local club or organization wanting to increase its membership with new blood. The Locomotive Society and the Development Corporation soon got together with the local council to see if a permanent base could be found for a 'steam museum'. There were a few hurdles to overcome, but the enthusiasm needed for success was there. By 1972 the Peterborough Locomotive Society changed its name to the Peterborough Railway Society, and then decided that its main aim should be to bring the Nene Valley Railway back to life, serving the interests of a much wider community.

You will appreciate that I am only sketching in very briefly the main details of a more complicated history. A lot of hard work went on behind the scenes to bring these ideas to reality. Help and financial support came from a variety of sources over the years, but without the labour and dedication of volunteers the Nene Valley Railway would not have survived. The man whose dream was coming true was himself no stranger to the footplate, the oil-can, or ticket-selling. Even so, an enormous amount of sweat and time from others was needed to make it a success, and many people deserve recognition. I will mention but three: Peter Waszak, David Smith and Brian White.

In order to convince our friend Stephen that trains do actually run along that track I decided to take a trip one Saturday morning, so that I would have a ticket and some photographs to prove its existence. It could not have been a more perfect day. The early-morning frost was soon dissolved by the warm October sun, and the forecast for the rest of the day was good. I decided to phone the station just to make sure that the first train of the morning was running this late in the season. Instead of the dehumanized speaking timetable that one gets these days on mainline services, there was a real live human voice at the other end which said: 'Yes, sir, the 11.20 a.m. to Peterborough leaves at 11 o'clock, because it goes to Yarwell first and then comes back to Wansford to pick up anyone who may have missed it. And, if I might say so, sir, it is worth going as far as Yarwell, because you get a good view of the trout lakes.'

The 11.20 from Wansford

I made sure that I was going to catch the 11 o'clock by asking my wife to drive me to the station by 10.45, offering in return to do some shopping in town on my way home. I walked up the steps to the booking hall and ticket office, where I bought a single fare to Peterborough. The man on duty behind the window looked disappointed and said 'Are you sure you only want one way, sir?' 'Quite sure,' I replied. 'I want to see what it's like first.'

The train was already in and quite full. An announcement over the public-address system informed me that 'the train now standing on platform 2 will be calling at Ferry Meadows, Orton Mere, and Peterborough'. I noticed that there was a First Class carriage and asked the guard if I was entitled to use it on my single ticket. He said that the N.V.R. made no distinction, because it was 'not worth the hassle'. I noticed that the bar was already doing a good trade but made my self-righteous way to the first-class compartment – which it probably was, *once*. Nevertheless, it still felt good to be travelling in faded luxury without having to pay for the privilege.

At two minutes past eleven there was a frantic flurry of brown smoke and a few dragon-like snorts of steam, and we began to move. The laboured grunting of the shunter engine gave the impression that we were being hauled forward in jerks by some heavy-breathing ox. About eighty per cent of the passengers were children, and they sounded as excited as if they had just experienced lift-off to the moon. We paused at the scenic prospect of the trout lakes, which I soon figured out was where we had to wait while the engine changed ends to take us back to Wansford to pick up those passengers who had missed the train in the first place.

Looking out of the window I saw a huge cloud of black smoke momentarily eclipsing the sun and the trout lakes; then we puffed off once more in the direction from which we had just come. When we got to Wansford I could see, by sticking my head out of the window, that we were in fact changing engines. Even that simple action reminded me of one of the things we have lost in our high-speed, safety-proof trains of today: you can't put your head out of the window to see what is happening (which, at 130 miles an hour, is just as well).

The guard waved his green flag, blew his whistle, adjusted his gold-braided cap, and off we went again through the Nene Valley. This time there was a much healthier *chuff, chuff* from the larger engine and we began to pick up speed. As I listened to the rhythm of the wheels I began to realize how many of the noises and smells of the old steam trains I had forgotten. Soon I was recalling those sepia-coloured journeys to Hunstanton. I could see the stuffy carriages with their sagging luggage-racks, smell the acrid smoke from the engine, feel the sting in my eye as a hot smut blew in through the window – and always someone in the compartment peeling an orange. Outside, the telegraph wires bounced up and down as the Fens gave way to Norfolk and then the sea.

Looking out of the window of my faded first-class compartment last Saturday morning I was surprised at how gentle and lovely this part of the country can be. As we approached Ferry Meadows the train appeared to glide through a glade of silver birches, maple trees, and bushes weighed down with red berries. The River Nene was flashing with sunlight, fat sheep were grazing in the fields, and a heron flew a few yards away from where we had disturbed him.

At Ferry Meadows we picked up another thirty passengers and slowly set off on the remainder of our journey. I waited for the engine's whistle to blow. It did, with the same evocative magic that I had heard so many times from my home. So, Stephen, I can assure you that it is *not* a tape-recording.

The next station was Orton Mere, where a few more passengers joined the train. The track now passed through some very attractive autumn scenery which, at times, was so dense and wild that one could easily have believed that we were travelling through jungle country on some faraway continent. Would there be tigers soon, or crocodiles? Sadly not. What we saw next were houses, factories and reminders of the twentieth century. Within minutes we were pulling into Peterborough and the terminal for Railway World. My romantic journey was over, and I was more than satisfied with the adventure.

As I walked away from the age of steam to make my way into the city and its shops, a sleek GNER electric train slithered almost silently over the bridge which crosses the Nene, and I have to admit that it did look rather grand and sophisticated. But, I wondered, will there be anyone in fifty years time who will be sufficiently nostalgic about these modern trains to form a society that will preserve something of what it was like to travel by rail in the last decade of the millennium? Maybe – though I doubt if it will be quite the same. As I implied earlier, it is more than the trains that makes us wistful. My wistfulness was soon to be shattered, though, because ten minutes later I was caught up in the frantic Saturday crowds of a city and felt like a ghost from the past. The rush, noise, rudeness and pressure of the age seemed too much. But I had promised to do the shopping, so I put on an old-fashioned stiff upper lip.

I was relieved to get home, to settle down again for the after-noon and listen to that distant, beguiling sound that would come like 'the notes of a bird in a forest' and put its final haunting cadence on the day's amusement. Experience has taught me that it is best to keep the past at a safe distance, rather like a train's whis-tle. My trip had simply been a pleasant distraction from reality which I enjoyed very much.

However much one might wish to, one cannot go back to a place or a time and expect everything to be the same – or as one frequently and inaccurately thinks it used to be. As Albert Camus said in his essay 'Return to Tipasa': 'It is sheer madness to return to the sites of one's youth and try to relive at forty what one loved or keenly enjoyed at twenty.'

I must admit now that I was never mad about trains as a boy, and the only Hornby train-set I had as a child received rough treatment at my hands, which always wanted the engine and tin carriages to travel at unacceptable speeds. I suppose all this harking back is something to do with our search for some kind of innocence. It's not so much the steam trains that we mourn, it's our youth.

✺ 21 ✺

A Few Old Chestnuts

It would not surprise me to learn that one of the most frequently quoted lines of poetry at this time of the year is the one written by John Keats nearly two hundred years ago: 'Season of mists and mellow fruitfulness …'. And I think I am brave enough to say that maybe not everyone who quotes it would be as sure of the line which follows, 'Close bosom-friend of the maturing sun'. When we get to autumn, though, the beginning of that poem is one which, for most of us, still expresses the true feeling of nature imposing its own calm mood of resignation and fulfilment in unmatchable beauty.

The line is so well-known it gets parodied more than most. I know someone who can be relied upon at the beginning of October to say, 'Season of coughs and old rheumatic pains / Close bosom-friend of the maturing man' – which at least proves that a line needs more than the correct metre to make it poetry. Not that he means any irreverence to the original poem, or to poor Keats, who died of tuberculosis in Rome at the age of twenty-six.

Autumn is both a real season in nature and the symbol of a season in our lives when we may feel ourselves fading a little, like the leaves on a tree. But it is also a time of celebration, the time of harvest festivals and St Luke's little summer. I am actually writing to you on St Luke's Day – 18 October – and it could indeed be summer. We have been able to sit out in the garden in summer clothes and feel the warmth of the sun as if we had somehow slipped back into August. (In some ways it was better, because the warmth of the October sun was less fierce than that of the brasher days of August.) It is surprising how regularly St Luke's Day produces this late warm spell, which lingers like a reluctant leave-taking of the summer we have taken for granted. It is in every sense a season of mists and mellow fruitfulness, and many other poets have been at their best when writing about autumn.

When I went out first thing this morning it was quite foggy, and the trees were hardly visible. The fields were covered in small cobwebs glassy with dew, and there were hundreds of tiny white mushrooms which were not there the night before. Yet, within an hour, the sun was trying to break through, like warm breath huffed on to the sky's cold window. I was reminded of the burning-glass I had as a boy, of how it slowly burnt a hole in a piece of rag or paper. The magic of heat; the mystery of fire. It is hard to believe that our sun is no more than a dying spark in the greater galaxies of the universe. To me it is immortal, life-giving and wonderful. Without it we wouldn't exist, and we spend a great deal of our time seeking it even though we now know that too much exposure to its rays can be harmful.

By mid-morning it had completely dispersed the mist, and I could see the glory of the October trees, especially the limes and chestnuts – always the first to turn, just as they are the first to come into leaf. The chestnuts especially had shed their season of fruitfulness a couple of weeks ago, and scores of conkers lay strewn on the paths and across the road, where passing traffic squashed them to pulp.

When I was a boy the conkers didn't stay there long enough to be squashed. We were out with our buckets, bags, cardboard boxes, or just large pockets, collecting them in their hundreds for our autumn sport. We didn't always wait for them to fall. We would throw stones or sticks up into the branches, hoping to knock down some of the green gems we could see hanging there, plump and spiky, destined for our conker championships in the playground and some kind of immortality. We were probably told it would have been wise to leave them there on the bough – to let them fall in their own time, for not until then were they truly ripe – but we dared not risk waiting for that to happen in case a rival boy got there before us.

We didn't have far to go for our conkers, because there were chestnut trees and walnut trees in the field next to the church at the end of our street, and when we had stripped those there were others nearby at Briggate Bridge. There was always something very special about breaking open the thick, fleshy shells, revealing that never-before-seen slimy white and brown nut; it was like being at the birth of a calf or foal. The nut was sweetly sticky, yet smooth as silk, unblemished and innocent. Each one was held like a precious stone in the hand, to be admired, polished, envied, coveted and finally fought over. At the moment of receiving such a gift no one would have thought that within days, if not hours, some of those conkers would be threaded on to leather shoe-laces or strong string and used as instruments of war, bashing one's opponents' prize conkers to smithereens, or seeing one's own tragically demolished by a one-time friend.

There were various ways of cheating, of making the conkers harder than nature intended. Some boys soaked theirs in very salty water, others baked theirs in the oven, some slept with them under their pillows or rubbed them with linseed oil. These were myths more than remedies, and the real skill came in knowing how to hit your opponent's conker in the right place. To have a conker that had knocked out fifty others put you in the premier league; there were those who boasted of a hundred victories, though mine never survived that long. Some conkers never even went into battle, but were threaded on to longer pieces of cord, so that they became a garland of large, bright beads fit for an Indian chief.

When I see so many conkers lying ungathered on the ground these days, I wonder if boys have lost interest in such simple games, but perhaps they collect theirs elsewhere, far from busy roads and traffic noise. Or have computer games taken over completely? I am happy to tell you, however, that the game has not died out altogether, at least not for adults. Not far from Peterborough is the tiny village of Ashton, where each year the Pearl World Conker Championships are played out in front of hundreds of spectators. This year I believe there was even the fear that there would be a shortage of conkers, because of the weather – the drought earlier in the year had not helped to produce a vintage crop. But you can't let such an important international sporting event not take place, and in the end more than enough good conkers were gathered for the organizers to select the 1,500 needed for the tournament.

This unique event was started in 1964 and has attracted competitors from all over the world – France, South Africa, New Zealand, Italy, Germany, Norway and America. There are various classes, one for adults, one for juniors and one for ladies. This year more than 330 competitors came to take part, and the organizers were hoping to raise more than £15,000 for charity. It was a lovely October day as the village prepared for its invasion. Usually the *Chequered Skipper* inn is the place to meet old friends, but last year the poor

Chestnuts at Ashton

old 'butterfly' was burnt down – nothing to do with the conker contest – and so a marquee had to take its place. The magnificent trophy for the men's section was won by a Mr Paul Vjestica (from Peterborough, of course), who beat the Frenchman Francis Vieillemard. One or two competitors certainly seemed anxious to regain their youth despite being nearly eighty years old. And why not!

We have come to look upon the horse-chestnut tree as very English, because it looks so at home on our village greens, near our churches or in our parks, but it was not introduced into this country until the late sixteenth century, and another two hundred years were to pass before the nuts were used for the game of conkers. Before that snail-shells were used for a similar type of game – hence the word 'conker', which owes its origin to the French word *conque*. The herbalist Gerard tells us in his *Herball* (1597) that the horse-chestnut tree was so called because 'the people of the East countries do with the fruit thereof cure their horses of the cough'. So, when you think of it, it is a remarkably versatile and interesting tree all the year round, from its first sticky buds and waxy blooms of spring to its spiky conkers and brilliant displays of dying leaves in autumn. Our landscapes, whether rural or urban, would be impoverished without them.

And now back to St Luke's little summer. Sitting in the garden after lunch we watched a pair of magpies competing with a couple of squirrels to entertain us with their displays of acrobatics. We are not very happy at the thought of magpies spending the winter with us. We already have a pair of sparrow-hawks nearby, so the smaller birds that we do encourage will be doubly threatened next spring; if the magpies don't get their eggs, the hawks will no doubt pick off the fledglings, if they have the chance. As we have wrens, blue tits, great tits and dunnocks as well as robins and blackbirds, we do not wish to see them scared off by further predators.

All the same, one cannot deny that the magpie, with its very distinctive plumage and behaviour, is a striking bird to watch. More and more it is finding the courage, or perhaps the need, to venture into suburban areas, and townspeople are as superstitious about it as country folk. Most of us have heard the saying 'one for sorrow, two for joy', and there is a variation on this in the old rhyme:

> One's for sorrow, two's for mirth,
> Three's a wedding, four's a birth.

In some country areas people would spit three times over the right shoulder, or raise their hats if they saw only one bird. In Scotland, I believe, if a magpie flies across the window of a house it is a sign of death, and in Sweden the bird is still associated with witchcraft.

The squirrels were finally intimidated by the magpies and trapezed away through our neighbour's trees, leaving the newcomers to show off their black-and-white costumes against a backdrop of yellow and red autumn leaves. It was like watching the well-measured moves in a game of draughts.

With this season of fruitfulness inevitably comes the flurry of harvest festivals. From the illustrations I have seen and the descriptions I have read, I have always believed this custom to be deeply rooted in three or four hundred years of rural history, but as a church festival, it goes back only to the nineteenth century, when, on 1 October 1843, the Reverend R.S. Hawker, vicar of Morwenstow in Cornwall, set aside that Sunday in order that his parish could thank God for a good harvest. Gradually the idea caught on in the rest of the Church until it became an established feature of the ecclesiastical calendar, so it was not long before congregations up and down the land were singing

> Come, ye thankful people, come;
> Raise the song of harvest home!
> All is safely gathered in,
> Ere the winter storms begin.

Those words made me realize why I was confused. There is a difference between 'harvest festival' and the much older, secular, custom of 'harvest home'; in the old days of gathering in the harvest by hand, the farm labourers sang the last load of corn out of the fields and then celebrated with beer and supper, usually provided by the farmer as a thanksgiving. So, in a way, I am justified in thinking that harvest festivals have been with us for a long time, and I could say, with a villager I once met, that 'they've celebrated harvest as long as I can remember'.

Whatever its origins, I am sure that most communities respond to the appeal, trappings, expectations and fun of modern harvest festivals, when our churches are decorated with flowers, fruits and vegetables to show how well we have been provided for by man and nature. A couple of weeks ago I helped to take part in the harvest festival at Soham, near Ely. I had been asked to run a writers' workshop with a group of children. We met in the church on the Saturday morning, in the expectation that we could create a sequence of harvest poems which could be read in the service on Sunday. The result was more than satisfactory. The boys and girls produced some excellent poems; although they had grown up in the age of the combine harvester and modern technology, they were still able to write about the old magic of harvests their grand-parents would have known, as well as about the more efficient methods of their own age. They, too, were part of an undying tradition of 'bringing in the sheaves' and knew how to celebrate the annual gifts of the earth. By the end of the morning we had several poems that were worthy of being read in anyone's harvest festival and the church itself was looking splendid with all its flower arrangements and displays of produce.

Soham is the oldest religious site in Cambridgeshire, and the present church has been a place of Christian worship for more than eight hundred years. St Felix, the first bishop of the East Angles, founded a monastery here in the seventh century and was later buried here in AD 647; his relics eventually being moved to the abbey at Ramsey. The earliest record of a parish priest, though, is in 1219, when Ranolph was appointed as the guardian of Soham. During our lunch-time break I had the pleasure of meeting the present incumbent, the Reverend Michael Shears, and within minutes we were enjoying a conversation about some of the Church's well-known priests who were also poets – John Donne, George Herbert, Thomas Traherne and R.S. Thomas. We were soon able to agree that the gentle George Herbert was perhaps the greatest Christian poet the Church had produced, even though the Jesuit Gerard Manley Hopkins earned our respect for his originality and brilliant use of language.

I drove home knowing that this season of mists and mellow fruitfulness was a very satisfying time of year and that harvests could be gathered in from many different fields. We may not have the old harvest sheaves any more, but the earth's offerings will always be worthy of our praise and thanksgiving.

Looking back over what I have just written it suddenly occurs to me that in all the displays of harvest produce I have seen in churches over the years I have never seen a dish or bowl of conkers.

Now how on earth can we omit the fruit of the chestnut tree from our annual celebrations? Perhaps we should have a special 'Conker Sunday'.

22

A Retreat at Madingley

I think you would have enjoyed my weekend – that's if stepping back some four hundred years in time appeals to you. In fact I am sure that, if you could have seen the beautiful house where I was staying, and the gardens that surround it, you would not have wanted any persuasion.

Before I make you too envious, I should explain that this was a working weekend, and not some luxury holiday I had won. Nevertheless, when the place of work is as stately as Madingley Hall, near Cambridge, one has no cause to complain about working for the privilege.

For the past few years I have been invited by my friend Trevor Hold to share a course with him at Madingley for the University of Cambridge Board of Continuing Studies – sometimes in the spring, but this year in the autumn. The subject is always the same – Poets and Composers – with different sets of poets and composers each year, of course. The aim of these courses is to study the close but often complex relationship (or, if you prefer, marriage) between English poetry and English music. Without either we would not have that rich heritage of English song. So it is appropriate that we can pursue this interesting subject in such a beautiful setting.

Not all poets like to have their poems set to music, and more than a few tetchy relationships have developed because some composers have taken liberties with the words and upset the author in the process. A E Housman did not like the idea and seldom approved of what he heard, yet he has been set by several different composers, so much so that his poems are known more now as songs. I remember reading his 'Bredon Hill' in public some years ago, and at the end of the concert a lady came up to me and said 'I had no idea that that song made such a good poem'. There was no such confusion with our students at Madingley.

There were, I might add, moments when Trevor and I wondered if we would ever get to Madingley. Friday afternoons are not the best times to be on the A1 and A14, especially with all the massive road improvements that are going on there at present. But when an oil-spillage from a tanker two miles ahead brings the traffic to a standstill, one's frustration is stretched to the point of nervous breakdown (at least mine was, because I had asked Trevor for a lift, and this had put him on a different route from the one he would normally have chosen). Our only consolation was the spectacular display of hundreds of starlings whirling and leaping in their sundance ritual (not that they could see any sun, but for them it was the hour of roosting). They were like a great black shawl of smoke tossed up by the wind, a huge handful of seeds thrown by some immortal sower, not knowing where they would fall, on tree-top or furrow.

We sat and waited as the minutes ticked by, as the sky slowly darkened and the birds became no more than a drifting smudge above the wet fields. What should have been less than an hour's journey took us just over two hours. And with the darkness came fog, which now made the rear-lights in front of us appear wrapped in gauze. I think anyone in our position would have been eager to leave the twentieth century with all its noise, confusions, bottlenecks and stagnating progress. It was with inexpressible relief that we drove through the iron gates and up the tree-lined drive that led us back to the sixteenth century and a sudden air of tranquillity that Madingley guarantees.

Madingley Hall is an elegant, imposing building with its corner towers, high windows and decorative brickwork, and it is equally impressive within. The hall is surrounded by formal gardens and parklands which slope away from the buildings, giving the impression that it is built on a hill. The earliest parts of the house date from 1543, with further important additions during the next fifty years, and more in the 1700s. It was originally built by Sir John Hynde as a hunting lodge, but eventually became the family's main residence. The Hyndes owned Madingley until 1647, when Jane Hynde, the sole heiress, married Sir John Cotton, a wealthy landowner and baronet. The property then passed into his family and underwent further alterations. It was, however, Sir John's grandson who was responsible for most of the major restoration of the house and for redesigning the gardens. For the next two centuries the house's fortunes were to fluctuate, and later generations were not to prove as conscientious about their inheritance. The sixth baronet lost most of his money through gambling and Madingley Hall passed to his sister, Lady King.

One chapter of the Hall's history which always attracts attention concerns Edward Prince of Wales (later Edward VII), who lived at Madingley when he was an undergraduate at Cambridge. He was never the most serious of students and was well-known in the area for his high living and fondness for women. His father, Prince Albert, found it necessary to visit him on more than one occasion to tick him off about his scandalous behaviour, the last time to remonstrate with him about his affair with an Irish actress. After this the Hall continued to decline and was then sold to a Mr Hurrell, who neglected his newly-acquired property to such an extent it was in danger of becoming a ruin. (Had that happened I would certainly not be writing to you now about my weekend there.) In 1905 it passed to a new and more responsible owner, Colonel Walter Harding, who immediately put into operation a costly programme of restoration which was to continue until the First World War. Afterwards the estate passed to his son Ambrose and then to Ambrose's daughter Rosamund.

In 1947 the Hall, with its gardens, outbuildings, parklands, entrance lodge, six farms, twenty-one cottages, the *Three Horseshoes* public house, the village hall and blacksmith's shop, were bought by the University. The Hall and adjoining buildings were converted into a hostel for graduates during term time and, during the vacations, a residential centre for adult education courses organized by the then University Board of Extra Mural Studies. In 1975 the Hall became the Board's headquarters and a full-time residential centre for adult students throughout the year. That is how Trevor and I came to be there again, working with a group of mature students from many different parts of the country and a variety of backgrounds, all of whom had come to this magnificent place in pursuit of knowledge and a glimpse of history.

As you can imagine, the Hall is now in an immaculate state, and the interior offers a collection of excellent rooms for lectures, study groups, social gatherings and relaxation. The dining hall is especially impressive, with its Jacobean plaster mouldings, carved panelling, portraits and high decorated windows which overlook the front terrace. To assemble in that candle-lit room for one's first meal is a memorable experience, especially after an awful journey. It quickly conditions one for the rest of the weekend, and, from the moment that the Warden says the Latin Grace and the first course is served, the appalling pressure of traffic on the A1 and A14 is already fading into its own soulless history, a history that one doesn't have to rejoin for at least another thirty-six hours.

I am not going to burden you with a detailed account of our academic activities during the weekend, but I ought at least to try to convince you that our programme was a very full one. The first session with our group of students was immediately after dinner – not the most conducive time of day to begin serious study. We met, as usual, in the Stuart Room and presented our introduction to the poets and composers we had chosen for this year's course – William Blake, John Clare and W B Yeats, with the musical settings composed by Benjamin Britten, Vaughan Williams, Ivor Gurney, Peter Warlock and Trevor Hold.

What I would prefer to do now is to give you a few more descriptions of the house and the gardens which have been developing mainly during the last 250 years. It is not clear whether there were any formally laid out gardens when the Hall was first used as a hunting lodge, but an engraving by J Kip based on a drawing by L Knyff in 1705 does show a Dutch-style design of avenues and squares, the kind of garden that was fashionable during the reign of William III. However, this was destroyed in 1756, when the famous Lancelot 'Capability' Brown was engaged to create new gardens, for which he received a fee of £500. He replaced the rigid Dutch look with a lawn and gravel path, planted hundreds of new trees, built ornamental ponds and opened up vistas to the sloping meadows beyond.

Regrettably, as the years passed Brown's creations, like the Hall itself, were neglected by subsequent owners, and there are only a few signs left of 'Capability's' achievements. The gardens were redesigned yet again by Colonel Harding at the beginning of the twentieth century, with an imaginative variety of plants and trees to complement those which had survived. His son was eager to carry on the good work and later created the topiary garden, still one of the most popular features of Madingley Hall.

When I woke on the Saturday morning there had been a sharp frost, and it was still foggy. Every bush, twig, branch and tree was silver-coated and perfectly still, as if frozen in time, waiting for some far-off spring or genesis to bring the world back to life. I

North wing of Madingley Hall

walked out before breakfast and took some photographs, then rejoined the rest of the group.

By mid-morning the autumn sun had eased its way through the fog enough to give the buildings a pale golden glow. By lunch time there was only a thin mist hanging like fine fluff over the grass, and the light on the brickwork was now the colour of ripe apricots. After lunch I went for a walk into the walled garden. There was no one else about, and it could have been the herb garden of a secluded monastery, far removed from the modern world – a good place to think, to prepare one's mind for the next session on John Clare.

The University's Board of Continuing Education, as it is now called, organizes more than two hundred residential courses a year, ranging from music, literature, art, creative writing and ancient history, to management studies and the training of professional groups in industry, commerce, law and the media. Consequently, a few thousand people each year have the benefit of staying in an historic and beautiful house to which they would not otherwise have access. That in itself is an enhancement of whatever other education they are receiving during their few days there. The student accommodation is of a high standard with well-equipped *en suite* rooms and a comfortable bar in which to relax after an exhausting day's study.

Not far from the mellow peace of Madingley Hall is a place where you will find peace of another kind – the poignant, numbing peace (or rather price) of war. I refer to the American Military Cemetery, with its silent crescents of white crosses, row upon row: the 3,811 graves of young men from across the Atlantic who came over to help liberate Europe from the tyranny of the Nazis and died doing it. The roll-call on the massive Wall of the Missing records a further 5,125 names of servicemen whose graves are unknown. Here, on the hushed and sanctified soil of an English field, is the chilling reminder of what peace costs.

From the steps of the cemetery's Memorial Chapel one can look out across the autumn landscape and, on a clear day, see Ely Cathedral sixteen miles away. So much history separates the two places, and yet they are also united in those struggles for something better than hatred and oppression. I have visited most of the War Cemeteries in France and Belgium, too, and I always feel too choked with anger, sorrow, pity and shame to say anything – one walks silently away, anaesthetized by the scale of such a sacrifice. In a few days time, now, we shall be wearing our red poppies, standing in small groups around our village war memorials, or watching on television the national pageantry of Remembrance Sunday. We shall be shown again the acres of white headstones, the poppies blowing in Flanders fields, and hear the Last Post sounded from village greens to the Cenotaph, and even from the very scenes of those now historic battles. We shall be shown the fading photographs of those husbands and sons which have been kept on sideboards or bedside tables for eighty years, or maybe fifty if the men were casualties of the Second World War. How can we fail to be moved? To hear suggestions that such a time of remembrance should be discontinued before we reach the millennium is a sad reflection of how insensitive and ungrateful some people have become in the twilight of this tragic century.

Our weekend at Madingley came to an end far too soon. When Trevor and I left after lunch on Sunday the fog was already forming again, denser than the day before, so we were hoping that there would not be any more traffic hold-ups to prevent our getting home before dark. Despite missing an important temporary slip-road on the A1, we just about made it. And what were we talking about on the homeward journey? Which poets and composers to choose for our next course at Madingley in 1999! And would we go for the autumn again, or decide that next time it should be spring? Well, there will be many more leaves to fall before then, and who knows where we'll be.

In the meantime, I have to come back down to earth and am getting on with the book I am supposed to have finished before Christmas. And you know only too well how all the preparations for that celebration can consume days of normal time before it arrives. But is that a tradition we would also agree to dispense with? I doubt it.

࿇ 23 ࿇

Stalking the Ghost of William Cobbett

I am looking out of my window this morning at a spotless blue sky which is so bright and clear that I could easily be peering into a deep lake of pure water. There is not a fleck of cloud in sight, no vapour trails from invisible aircraft, no smoke from a neighbour's bonfire, not even a ripple on the surface from the flight of a bird. Everything is very still, as if the November sun had carefully stuck each yellow leaf, each bush, tree and building into place like photographs fixed in an album.

You would think that such a peaceful moment would make me contented. It does in a way, and I am grateful for it, but it also makes me restless. I am torn. I want to sit here enjoying these quiet moments, but I also long to be out in the Fens, where this restricted view becomes a reality. I would go if I were not so far behind with my work, and I know that it would not take much persuasion from my other self to make me put down my pen, put on a sweater, get in the car, and dash out to Welney or to Wingland for some fresh air. I have learned from past experience that it often pays to give in to this kind of temptation. Very often the unexpected happens. I have always believed in putting oneself in the way of adventure and taking what comes. But today I do not have the courage to desert the pages of manuscript waiting to be typed, or the mountain range of letters still to be answered, so I had better shut my eyes to the seductive, shining, beckoning day outside and convince myself that at the day's end a clear conscience will be easier to live with than the thought of a morning wasted because of self-indulgence.

On the other hand, days like this will soon be all too rare. When the winter sets in I shall probably regret not taking advantage of such a morning. Then pull yourself together, I say, and go out while you can. You can make time for the work in some other way. It will keep.

So, with that brief argument over, I have made the decision to leave my desk and this Letter for the time being. The call of freedom has won, and I feel sure that by the time I return I shall have something more interesting to say to you. Does that make me weak-willed and undisciplined?

Later that day: Do you remember how those succinct captions were used so effectively in the days of silent movies – '*Next morning* . . .', or '*The following year* . . .'? They saved pages of boring narrative having somehow to be translated into visual terms. I can't promise the same brevity in this resumed Letter, but it will be clear to you now that I did not chain myself like some doomed hero to the railway track, or my desk. I went in search of whatever the day had waiting for me and found myself heading into Lincolnshire and eventually Holbeach. I took my usual route through Crowland, Gedney Hill, Holbeach Drove and Holbeach St Johns – roads which take the traveller over a landscape of silent fields and a network of waterways that make this part of England unmistakable Fen country. The South Holland Main Drain, which discharges itself into the River Nene on its last lap to The Wash, is an impressive piece of drainage which, on a day like today, can look as majestic as any natural river.

When I am driving across the Fens I can't help but think of some of those earlier travellers who came here and wrote of their impressions in letters, journals and essays – Samuel Pepys, Daniel Defoe, William Cobbett and Hilaire Belloc among them.

It was Cobbett, in particular, whom I thought of today as I made my way to Holbeach. In the spring of 1830 he travelled through most of the Fen country, staying at several towns where he addressed large and sometimes hostile audiences on the state of agriculture, social reform and politics. To give you some idea of how active and tireless he was in his travels, let me quote his itinerary for one week in the April of that year.

On 2 April he spoke at the Playhouse in Peterborough, where, he tells us, 'it snowed all day' and was 'very wet and sloppy'. But he still attracted 'a good large audience' and did not let the opportunity pass 'without telling my hearers of the part their good neighbour, Lord Fitzwilliam, had acted in the French War'.

On 3 April he was at the Playhouse in Wisbech, speaking to 220 people. He then stayed the night at Sutton St Edmunds and, as the following day was Sunday, stayed a further night, during which there was such a hard frost that on the Monday morning he woke to find 'ice an inch thick' and a 'total destruction of the apricot blossom'. (I was a bit puzzled to read of apricots growing in the Fens and wondered if he was referring to some other fruit.) Later that day he travelled to Crowland, where in the evening he met a 'very large assemblage of the most respectable farmers'. The following day he was in King's Lynn addressing an audience of over 300 people where 'there was more interruption than I have ever met with in any other place'.

This tall and robust man was an accomplished horseman, undeterred by distance or weather. The essayist William Hazlitt described him as 'tall and portly' with a 'good, sensible face and ruddy complexion'. He was 'mild in his manner, deliberate and unruffled in his speech ... and wore a scarlet broadcloth waistcoat, with the flaps of the pockets hanging down, as was the custom for gentlemen farmers'.

On 8 April Cobbett was in Holbeach in 'this noble county of Lincoln' and was clearly very impressed by what he saw. He felt at home with hard-working farmers. His father was a peasant farmer near Farnham in Surrey and never had more than a few pence to spare. Looking back on his childhood William Cobbett was to recall:

> I do not remember the time when I did not earn my own living. My first occupation was driving the small birds from the turnip seed, and the rooks from the peas. When I first trudged afield, with my wooden bottle and my satchel slung over my shoulders, I was hardly able to climb the gates and stiles; and at the close of the day to reach home was a task of infinite difficulty. My next employment was weeding wheat and leading a single horse at harrowing barley ... My father used to boast that he had four sons, the eldest of whom was but fifteen years old, who did as much work as any three men in the parish.

Mr Cobbett senior taught his sons how to read and write, and when William was eighteen he decided to leave home and go to London to work as a copying clerk to an attorney. After a life in the open air he found the soulless drudgery of a city office more than he could bear, so he joined the Army as a common soldier in

the 54th Foot Regiment and later that year was posted to Nova
Scotia, then New Brunswick. During his service in America he met
the young woman who was to become his wife. In 1800 he
returned to England to pursue his career as a journalist and would-
be politician. But he was seldom out of trouble, and between 1802
and 1810 was twice tried and found guilty of libel on certain
members of the government. In 1810 he was back in court for the
second time that year on a charge of making accusations of the
Crown's approval of the public flogging of five militiamen. He was
sentenced to pay £1,000 – a very large sum of money in those days
– and to two years' imprisonment in Newgate jail. All this, and
much more, long before he got to Holbeach and the warm-hearted
local farmers.

I have taken the time to tell you this much about him to show
what an active, forthright and formidable man he was. Throughout
his life he edited the *Weekly Register*, farmed, travelled, lectured,
wrote numerous books and pamphlets, and eventually became a
Member of Parliament for Oldham. He died in June 1835 at the age
of seventy-three.

So what was it about Holbeach that made him praise it so highly
in 1830, and what was I going to find 167 years later? To answer
both these questions I must first of all give you a sample of what
Cobbett himself wrote:

Holbeach lies in the midst of some of the richest land in the world;
a small market-town, but a parish more than twenty miles across ...
produced an audience (in a very nice room, with seats prepared) of
178, apparently all wealthy farmers, and men in that rank of life; an
audience so deeply attentive to the dry matters on which I had to
address it I have very seldom met with. I was delighted with
Holbeach; a neat little town; a most beautiful church with a spire ...
gardens very pretty; fruit trees in abundance ... and land dark in
colour and as fine a substance as flour, as fine as if sifted through one
of the sieves with which we get the dust out of the clover seed; and
when cut deep into with a spade, precisely as to substance like a piece
of hard butter, yet nowhere is the distress greater than here.

Cobbett then goes on to compare the wealth of some with the
poverty of others, to see the fat sheep and hogs better fed and cared
for than the labouring people. He tells us that he could not help
exclaiming:

God has given us the best country in the world; our brave and wise and virtuous fathers, who built all these magnificent churches, gave us the best government in the world, and we, their cowardly and foolish and profligate sons, have made this once-paradise what we now behold!

It was mid-morning by the time I drove into town, and the streets were already busy with people shopping and others trying to park their cars. This sense of bustle, however, was quickly dispelled whenever I went into the shops. Admittedly I visited only three, but there was an air of old-fashioned courtesy and charm that I thought had disappeared altogether. The shopkeepers and assistants could not have been more patient, helpful and knowledgeable about their wares. (They were good salesmen too. I needed a new grey leather belt – which they did not have – and came out with two pairs of socks which my wardrobe did not require.) For such a small town – though I was told by one of the shopkeepers that Holbeach is still strictly only a village – there is an interesting variety of shops selling antiques, second-hand books, wine, flowers, perfumes, shoes and provisions. It even has a Boots *and* a Woolworths! I also saw at least six pubs on my brief walk, and nearly as many banks.

As I drove into Holbeach I was attracted to its large, fine church with a slender spire as sharp as a thorn. But would it be open? I walked up to its turreted porch, which was more like the gateway to a castle, and tried the door. Praise be, it opened, and I stepped inside to a very spacious building with a high roof. I thought I was alone until a lady glided, almost ghost-like, out of the shadows of the nave and decided to be my official guide.

'I like to come in every day for a few minutes, if I can, just to be by myself,' she explained. 'I don't like it so much when other people come here for the services, they spoil the atmosphere.'

She asked me where I was from and why I was there, but I kept it a secret. She almost took me by the hand to show me the beautiful wood-carvings on the lectern, then pointed to the two wooden angels just below the timber roof. 'Can you see, they're holding in their hands the nails from the crucifixion. . . . Every time I come here I get a message, a sign to show me that someone cares, but it hasn't happened today.'

I apologized and said that perhaps my arrival had spoilt it for her. 'Maybe,' she said quietly, 'or maybe you are it.' At that moment a shaft of sunlight pierced through the gloom and, like a theatre's spotlight, focused on her hand that rested again on a figure of Christ on the lectern. Her face beamed its own ecstatic, visionary smile and she said 'You see! He hasn't let me down after all. I need that kind of comfort because I'm looking after a very elderly relative and he's getting extremely difficult to handle. Why are old people so selfish?' Then she took my arm and led me to another part of the church.

We continued our tour until we were back at the west end and the altar-tomb of Sir Humphrey Littlebury. Sir Humphrey acquired land in Holbeach in the fourteenth century by marrying a local heiress, and he died when the church was being built more than 650 years ago. The effigy on the tomb shows him as a tall and slender knight in armour, with a broken sword, spurs and mail, his feet resting against what appears to be a lion.

From the way my mysterious lady touched everything, I could see that she loved every inch of the place. She told me that she had lived in Holbeach all her life and never wished to go anywhere else, not even for a holiday. I thanked her for her company and all the information she had given me, then stepped out once more into the busy street. Set in the church wall near the pavement is an old milestone which claims that from Holbeach it is 100 miles to London, 118 to Birmingham, 82 to Great Yarmouth and 23 to Peterborough – though my trip-gauge had recorded 26 miles on my way over. But I was glad to see the stone had been so preserved.

I crossed over the road to look at an exceptionally fine house which displayed a blue plaque. From it I learned that it was in this house that Sir Norman Angell was born in 1872. An author, lecturer and winner of the Nobel Peace Prize in 1933, he died in 1967. His was not a name I knew, but I discovered later that he wrote *The Great Illusion* (1908), which argued strongly against war; it sold over a million copies and was translated into twenty-five languages.

My impulsive decision to leave my desk and respond to the call of adventure had paid off, and, like the lady in the church, I hadn't been let down. As good fortune had followed me so far, I thought I would take advantage of the light and drive over towards the marshes. It is a strange, solitary region at the best of times. I have been out there in all weathers except a blizzard. The roads lead eventually to nowhere but the coastline of The Wash, that vast stretch of muddy water that not even winter sunlight can make sparkle. I made my way out through Holbeach Clough, Holbeach St Marks and

Holbeach St Matthew until I ran out of road, then walked another hundred yards or so towards what seemed to be the edge of existence. Although the light was still good, a chilly wind was now blowing in from the north, and when I felt that my brain's cobwebs had been blown away I strolled back to the car, where I sat and enjoyed the eternal power of nature from my modern metal cocoon.

I have mentioned on many occasions that this area of the Fen country is very different from the more inland areas. The land is different, and the sky is different. This is land for the wildfowler and naturalist. There is a sea smell, and it is a sea sky. The scene before you has no real horizon; earth melts into water, water blurs hazily into air. The view is limitless, timeless, awe-inspiring. Yet I know people who are terrified to be out here even on a beneficent day. They are terrified of the space and afraid of the silence.

My moments of peace were soon to be shattered when I decided it was time to make my way home and I had to cross the ghastly A17. It takes quite a time to recover, and I was well on my way to Holbeach Drove and Gedney Hill before I was able to relax again. The sun was now low in the sky, and its rays were gilding the reeds in the dykes: they could just have been sprayed with gold paint ready for Christmas, as some no doubt will be.

In the evening I had to give a talk in Peterborough to an audience of sixty farmers, their wives and guests, and felt not unlike William Cobbett as I warned them of the risks they were facing in the Fens as radical changes threatened their existence, such as those I have already mentioned in an earlier Letter to you – soil erosion, global warming, and urban sprawl.

Although there were farmers there from the high lands to the west of the Fens, like Sawtry and Stilton, most members of the audience were farming land below sea-level and were rightly concerned about the future of their farms. What could be done to prevent any of these tragedies happening? Several of them accepted that nature, in the end, usually wins the battle – especially as far as the weather is concerned – and it was now too late to put right the wrongs of earlier generations who had overdrained the Fens or had failed to see what would happen if peat soil was allowed to go on shrinking. There are now only small pockets of fen left in some areas, and the depth of peat is so shallow as to make the growth of some of the traditional crops impossible. One farmer told me it was years since he had grown any celery, and yet it used to be one of his main crops. Potatoes were threatened for the same reason, as was sugar-beet, and he wondered how much longer his family would be able to carry on farming land which had been theirs for over three hundred years. His air of resignation was shared by other Cambridgeshire men in the audience.

The Lincolnshire men were more concerned about what would happen if the earth's temperature did rise by the predicted 1.6°C within the next thirty years, thereby raising the sea-level, expanding the oceans and flooding 150,000 acres of fenland already below the plimsoll line. One jovial man said he would change to trout farming; another thought he would turn his farm into a marina. Others took a more optimistic view and believed that in our technological age there must be someone ingenious enough to design a defence system to prevent the rising waters from spilling over on to their low-lying land. One even thought he might make a fortune by piping all this surplus water to the desert, and a few just laughed, saying it was a lot of scare mongering and would never happen.

In fact it was the threat of urban sprawl that got them going on a more heated discussion. If the planned development of 14,000 acres of rural Cambridgeshire was going to produce another 150,000 or more new houses, where were the people going to work? *And* why build all these houses on land that was likely to be flooded? *And*, asked one man, what would all these newcomers know about the ways of the country, the true, traditional customs of country life that had been in existence for hundreds of years? The townee and the countryman have never seen eye to eye.

These questions inevitably led to the more controversial issues of fox-hunting, game-shooting and hare-coursing. A majority of the audience were against banning the hunt, nor did they want any curb put on their other country pursuits. One of the younger farmers stood up and said 'the trouble with letting all these townees in with their weird ideas of conservation and preservation is that they're more likely to upset the balance of nature than they are to protect it. They know very little about the subject anyway, and then try to tell us what we should or should not be doing on our own land.' It sounded as if we should soon need our own ombudsman.

As usual when you get a group of farmers together over a pint or two of beer, there was also a lot of banter and a swapping of anecdotes. Folklore and legends will never be dead whilst Fenmen can meet like this to tell their tales and tease each other. Whatever else might happen I hope these Fen-tigers will not lose their sense of humour.

It was getting on for eleven-thirty by the time I got home and I was tired, but it was that pleasant tiredness that comes from a day well spent. I wonder what this Letter would have been about had I not taken the same steps as Cobbett?

∼ 24 ∾
'In Housen and in Hall'

I don't suppose that I am alone in suffering from a pre-Yuletide panic, but the end of this year especially has caught up with me sooner than I would have wished. Trying to meet the deadline for completion of a book hasn't helped, and I feel particularly jittery when I remind myself that in three or four weeks time I shall be back to where this present volume began – celebrating the Whittlesey Straw Bear Day in January. However, like everyone else, I just have to accept that all the preparations now required for this frantic season will continue to play havoc with my normal orderly routine and placid temper.

Nevertheless, I tell myself, there will be some rewarding moments, such as receiving those Christmas cards from friends one very rarely sees, hearing the first carols whilst they are still fresh, and even buying the first easy presents. But against these unbruised pleasures will be the crush, rush, frenzy and frustration of the worst aspects of Christmas, especially in our large towns and cities, where a frenetic stare soon begins to take over the shoppers' smiling faces. Where, I ask myself, do all the people come from in these dervishing days of December? Each morning I see them arriving in coachloads, spilling out of the railway station or queueing in their cars for parking spaces that were taken up an hour ago.

But I will *not* be a modern-day Scrooge and say 'Bah!' and 'Humbug!' to Christmas, because I do still really enjoy it and like to make it as traditional as possible by adorning the house with plenty of evergreen and, when the dogs and cats are out of the way, decorating the tree. There are other joys too. For the past few years I have been invited in December to give a talk, or suitable reading, to the patients in the Sue Ryder Home at Thorpe Hall, Peterborough, as part of their Christmas activities. It is not an easy task, as I am now only too aware that for many of the residents there are very few Christmases left, and it is difficult to be jolly when each year I see a different group of faces from the year before. However, the Matron and her enthusiastic staff make absolutely sure that there is no cloud of doom hanging over the place. The Hall is beautifully decorated, there's the smell of hot mince-pies, and sometimes the sound of carol-singing, just as one imagines there always used to be in such an elegant house when it was privately owned.

As I drove up to the Hall, set in its very spacious and attractive grounds, it was just beginning to snow. The sky had been burdened with it all day, and a Siberian wind had harrowed the empty fields into that bleak mid-winter look. Snowflakes were already settling on the wings of the stone falcons at the main gate, and the house appeared shrouded in veils of fleece. But, as usual, there was a very warm welcome when I stepped inside, and one of the Sisters soon came to take me up to the magnificent drawing-room where I was to meet those patients who wanted, or were well enough, to hear me.

I think it might help to give you a better picture of the place if I told you a little about Thorpe Hall before it became a Sue Ryder Home. I remember going into it for the first time forty-five years ago, when it was used as a convalescent centre for the old Peterborough and District Memorial Hospital. My father was there recovering from an operation, and we joked about his being kept in such stately splendour. The history of the Hall is indeed very mixed and very complex, with periods of neglect and gloom as well as warmth, healing and joy.

It was built in 1653 by Lord Chief Justice Oliver St John, a wealthy lawyer and staunch supporter of Oliver Cromwell, into whose family he married when the Lord Protector's favourite cousin Elizabeth became his second wife. It was through these connections, and his controversial role as an ambassador in Holland, that St John acquired the Manor at Thorpe (now known as Longthorpe), together with the then ruined Minster at Peterborough (now the cathedral) which a few years before had been completely ransacked by Cromwell's troops. Surprisingly, and for whatever reason, he decided to present the remains of that ancient building as a gift to the citizens of Peterborough. Not, however, before helping himself to a large quantity of stone and timber for use in his new residence at Thorpe, which he was to call The Mansion House. More stone was also brought over from

Ketton, and the slate from Collyweston, both sources of the most durable building materials to be found in the area.

Oliver St John chose to build his mansion on what was the highest elevation in his manor, a modest hillock just above the River Nene meadows, which often flooded in winter. It was, and still is, a most imposing edifice on the outskirts of the city. But his dreams of grandeur were not to last long. He had flourished during the years of the Commonwealth, but those years were coming to an end; Cromwell's reign was over. By 1660 and the restoration of the monarchy, the safest place for any of that man's surviving followers who wished to avoid prison or the gallows, was to live abroad. Having defended himself with some success at his trial, receiving neither imprisonment nor execution, St John decided to leave England and retire to France, where he died on 21 December 1673.

His eldest son, Francis, then inherited the estate at Thorpe, but it was soon pointed out to him that his father's house had been built on land confiscated from the Dean and Chapter of Peterborough, and therefore either it should be surrendered or they should be suitably recompensed. Francis agreed to pay the sum of £1,500 and keep the house. During his time there he made several improvements to the property and the surrounding gardens. He also enlarged the library which his father had established, adding many more volumes on religion, politics, military history and the classics, until it became one of the most envied libraries in East Anglia.

Thorpe Hall remained in the St John family for two more generations and then passed through marriage to the Bernard family of Huntingdon, the town where Cromwell himself was born and went to school. Sir John Bernard, his wife Mary and their family moved into their new home in 1756, but they, too, were not to enjoy its comforts as long as they would have wished. Sir John died in 1766, and his estates went to his son Robert, a young man with a reputation for debauchery, decadence, debts and champagne. He installed his mistress at Thorpe Hall and subsequently sacked, or lost, most of his domestic staff, including his coachman and stable-boys. Robert died on 2 January 1789 with no heir to succeed him.

Eventually the entire contents of Thorpe Hall were sold at auction to help pay off some of the outstanding debts. Among some of the unusual items for sale were bows and arrows, firearms – including a pair of double-barrelled pistols mounted with silver – and thirty bottles of 'fine old rum'. Panelling was stripped from the rooms and marble fireplaces removed. The end of the

Bernards' era of ownership introduced the years of neglect and conflict that almost destroyed the Hall completely. In 1809 it became the property of the Fitzwilliam family but for the next forty years was to remain deserted until, in 1850, it was bought by the Reverend William Strong for £8,000, including the parklands. At that point it entered one of the happier chapters of its history.

William Strong, a wealthy and scholarly clergyman, lived at Stanground Manor on the south-east side of Peterborough, and so was close enough to supervise the restoration of the Hall during the next two years. No expense was spared. As well as extensive alterations to the house itself he replanted the gardens and built a conservatory. His first two wives had died whilst still young, and it was his third wife, Isabella Isham, who gave him the longed-for son, Charles Isham Strong, who inherited the Hall when his father died in 1855. Charles had a distinguished military career, and when he died in 1914 the Hall went to his son, another William, who also entered the Army and became a Brigadier-General. After the First World War he decided that he no longer wanted to own Thorpe Hall and put the house up for sale.

It was not everybody who could afford to buy and maintain such an estate, so it remained unsold, even at auction, for some time. Many improvements had been made, but it still had no electricity, no telephone and poor heating. The downstairs rooms were lit by oil-lamps or a few chandeliers, and the bedrooms had to rely on candles. The Hall was finally sold in 1927 for £11,500 to a Mr Edward Meaker, a London antiques dealer who wanted it not only as a house in the country but also as a showplace for his collection of rare antiques. The house had already changed its character. The oak doors, panelling, fireplace and books from the library had gone to Leeds Castle, and the rooms were as lifeless as an unfrequented museum.

Once again the Hall did not provide a long period of stability or comfort for its owners. Within ten years both Edward Meaker and his wife had died before their children came of age, and the house was left empty. During the Second World War it was requisitioned as a hospital, though it still remained part of the Meaker Trust. It was then leased to the Peterborough and District Memorial Hospital as a convalescent and rehabilitation centre until the new hospital was built, and Thorpe Hall's future again became uncertain. In 1975 it was bought by the Peterborough Development

Corporation, and in 1986 Lady Ryder acquired it for use as a Sue Ryder Home. That is where my own interest really begins to find its place in this Letter – although, when I think about it, my initial interest goes back to an experience I had nearly forty years ago in a different part of England.

I hope you won't mind if I digress once more to tell you about that, because it *is* connected and does have some bearing on my involvement with the Sue Ryder Foundation. In the mid-fifties a group of young writers who had frequently appeared in the same small literary magazines together decided to meet and form a more mutual and helpful circle of friends who shared one interest – getting our work published. One of the most talented and witty of that group was the poet Roye McCoye, already suffering from the severe disabilities of muscular dystrophy. He was twenty-nine and had known nothing of normal home life since his childhood; his mother died before he was ten years old, and his father died shortly after Roye had been moved to Greathouse, one of the Cheshire Homes established by Group-Captain Leonard Cheshire, Sue Ryder's husband. Greathouse was in the village of Kington Langley, near Chippenham, and one Easter another member of the group and I volunteered to go down for the weekend to help out in any way we could. The Matron gave us a pep talk and said 'whatever you do, don't feel sorry for the patients, otherwise they'll hate you. They are ordinary people with good brains but wonky bodies, and they like to feel independent.'

It could not have been a more beautiful weekend, with masses of daffodils, primroses, blue skies and endless laughter. On the Saturday evening we wheeled as many of the patients as we could up to the local pub, the *Hit and Miss*, and were determined to give them a good night out. The landlord willingly made room for the wheelchairs in the bar, where there was a piano, and we were soon enjoying an unforgettable evening of drinking, singing and telling stories (few of which could have been retold outside the pub). Watching those disabled people in various stages of physical deformity living it up with such gusto was an experience that taught me one of the most important lessons in my life. Not one of them was to see more than a few more years of life, but they did not let their illness inhibit their joy.

As well as writing poetry and short stories Roye was also editing his own literary magazine and compiling anthologies. He typed by touching the keys of his electric typewriter with a metal bar held in his mouth. When he could no longer type we corresponded through tape-recordings. He was always an inspiration and saw most of his work as a celebration of life. He died in 1964, aged thirty-four.

My visit to Greathouse made me realize how essential it is for such care to exist, and that sick people should be given that care in something more like a home than an institution. Greathouse was not unlike Thorpe Hall, a fine stone building that had once been a grand house, with elegant rooms, moulded ceilings and terraced gardens.

Many years later I was to read Lady Ryder's autobiography *A Child of Love* (1986) and was overwhelmed by her vision, courage, tenacity and her tireless service to others. Which brings me back to my visit to Thorpe Hall and one of the reasons why I am always delighted to be asked to do something for the patients there. I particularly enjoyed my afternoon again this year. One or two of the nurses were still putting trimmings up on the staircase, the Christmas tree was already lit, and there was a genuine festive atmosphere. Two or three of the patients also had relatives visiting them for the day, and they kindly joined in the discussion that eventually followed my initial presentation. I had read a few extracts from my autobiography *Fen Boy First*, choosing episodes in my own childhood with which I hoped they would be able to identify – Monday wash-days, Saturday bath-nights, and Christmas.

Christmas defies just ordinary nostalgia. It has a ritual, a richness and a folklore all of its own. Each year when I go to Thorpe Hall I hear memories of carol-singing, family parties and *snow*, as the patients recall their own childhoods and the kind of scenes that have been immortalized for us all in the literature of Thomas Hardy, Dylan Thomas and Laurie Lee. It always snowed; the lanterns always flickered in a chilly wind; the collection-boxes grew heavier with each call, and there were always those houses where the young carollers received their first hot mince-pie of the season, or bag of barley sugars. One patient said that when he was a boy in Yorkshire he and his mates would always spend their first well-earned 'thruppence' on a bag of roasted peanuts from the vendor outside the cinema. One of the ladies then told us that when she was a child the most exciting time at Christmas was the week or two before Christmas Eve. That was when she and her sisters used to search through every room and cupboard in the house trying to find where their parents had hidden the presents which they were meant to be surprised about on Christmas morning after Father Christmas had been ('Our brother had made quite sure we had long since ceased to believe in him'). Another patient said that whenever he thought of Christmas he remembered the smell of home-cured ham being sliced off the bone by his father. That made someone else remember the smell of home-made pickles and chutneys. 'And proper vegetables,' said another, 'grown in your own garden and not out of some supermarket freezer.' Soon all these memories led to laughter, and it was wonderful to see these people enjoying themselves, reliving those times when all was right with their world. One, who I knew to be very seriously ill, took my hand and murmured, 'I shall always be grateful for those good times. People are not so lucky today.'

From time to time I could not help glancing out of the large windows of the drawing room in which we sat and noticed that the gardens were fading into the shadows and the sky now darkening quickly towards evening. What changes this Hall had seen! Perhaps it was now experiencing the longest period of stability and comfort it had ever known.

With the formal part of the afternoon over the nurses arrived with trays of tea and mince-pies. It was only then that I realized that the Matron had been listening to us for most of the time, and I could see that she was pleased that some of the people in her care had been released for a while from the immediate fears about their future and would probably go on talking of other memories long after I had gone.

It was when they wished me a happy Christmas that I found myself lost for words. Somehow I felt that the real meaning of Christmas had been there in that room, in that Hall, where simplicity and grandeur sat side by side, where rich and poor would share in the love that this great event was all about. As I drove away from the Sue Ryder Home and back into the busy, noisy streets of a city seemingly intent on turning Christmas into a commercial success, I felt a stranger in a world where all the values had been turned the wrong way round. What was it really all about, this mad rush to eat, drink and be merry in a welter of gifts that would soon be forgotten, and in some cases were not even wanted: 'The sweet and silly Christmas things, / Bath salts and inexpensive scent / And hideous tie so kindly meant', to quote Sir John Betjeman? Or, as I once tried to put it:

Why is it there is always so much
preparation to celebrate the birth
of one for whom so little was prepared?
It never was intended that such
extravagance should change the worth
of one small gift meant to be shared.

For some it was enough to touch
the cradle, to stand on the cold earth
knowing that somewhere, someone cared.
Think now of that woman's search
for a bed, how she was left to writhe
in the damp straw, her cries unheard.

Today we follow the crowds who clutch
at the frayed hem of Mammon's cloth;
a costly remembrance to be endured.
Sometimes the star is beyond our reach
and we stare too long at an empty hearth
wondering why innocence has disappeared.

We'll strip the tree, take down the cards (each
dusty greeting is itself a death),
then burn their messages, word by word.
And is that all? Or shall we stretch
our hopes beyond the ashes' wreath
to wait for signs which cannot be ignored?

The miraculous snow that had greeted me as I arrived at Thorpe
Hall had now melted and turned to a fine rain. It was as if its magic
were no longer needed for the rest of the day.

Back in my own home I lit the fire, brought in another basket of
logs, then switched on the radio. Various personalities from the
world of politics and show business were being asked to name their
favourite carols. For some, I thought, this presented a difficult
choice, and when *I'm Dreaming of a White Christmas* was one of
the choices I couldn't help feeling that the question had been inter-
preted too liberally. Others, better informed, hesitated between *The
Holly and the Ivy* and *Silent Night*. Some chose *In the Bleak
Midwinter* or *The First Nowell*, and one said the most cheerful carol
of all was undoubtedly *Ding Dong Merrily on High*. Had I been
asked at that moment, I would probably have gone for *Deck the*

Hall with Boughs of Holly, though it is by no means my favourite. The one which I do like but seldom hear these days is *Three Kings from Persian Lands Afar*, and another which would have been appropriate is *As Joseph was A-walking*, with those simple but haunting lines:

> As Joseph was a-walking
> He heard an angel sing –
> 'This night shall be the birth-time
> Of Christ the Heavenly King.
>
> He neither shall be bornèd
> In Housen nor in Hall,
> Nor in a place of paradise,
> But in an ox's stall.'

My own preparations for Christmas received a sad interruption when I had a telephone call to say that my younger brother had died in Yeovil Hospital. He was sixty-two and for the past few years had suffered from the relentless edacity of multiple sclerosis. My youngest brother and his wife, with their son-in-law, took me down to Yeovil for the funeral, and on that long journey we had time to talk about the things we remembered most about the Christmases we had all shared as children. Again, it was not so much the presents we found in our pillow-cases on Christmas morning that came to mind as the family gatherings, party games, the sideboard loaded with bowls of fruit, nuts and port wine, and the awful jokes that came out for an airing each year. Later, at the funeral service, we heard our brother's oldest son say in a moving tribute to his father that, as children, they had been subjected to many of those jokes and had loved them too. I imagine that is how some relatives eventually become legends.

And so the night of the Nativity itself finally arrived. The shops at last closed their doors, emptied their tills, and the exhausted managers, check-out ladies and shop assistants went home to be with their families, to celebrate in their own way an event that changed the world, whether we believe in that Child of Love or not.

For all our doubts and personal confusions about the ultimate truth of it all, for all our sentimental attachments to a story that any questioning intellect finds hard to accept in every detail, there is still an aura of sublime mystery about Christmas. It is this that reawakens in us a moment of wonder, a glimmer of hope and a cheerfulness of spirit, as we remember that it all began because of one gift that was not asked for, was not even wanted, until its true value was revealed to shepherds, the three kings and the rest of the world. I know that many of our Christmas traditions have very little to do with its religious significance but if the manger, magi, angels and that strange bright star were suddenly removed from the script there would be a lot of people writing to the national newspapers to complain that something had been taken away from them that had always been theirs.

So where will the true spirit of Christmas be found this year? You know as well as I do that it will be found wherever people come together in sincerity to share in those acts of giving and receiving that express love and gratitude, not just for a year but often for a lifetime. It will be found in the humblest cottage or grandest hall, in a hospice or an apartment block, if the reason for our celebrations is allowed to shine upon us, and through us, for the sake of others.

It is good that at this dark time of the year we have three festivals so close together to keep our spirits up and give us renewed hope – Christmas, New Year, and Epiphany, which rounds off the season to perfection. Living in an increasingly violent society, which no one seems able to do anything about, we may sometimes wonder how the spirit of innocence and love can survive. It has to – otherwise we shall have surrendered to the barbarians and the thugs who believe in neither.

So, with this last Letter to you almost finished, I can do no more than wish you goodwill, good fortune, good health and much joy. I am now going to hang up my boots, if not my stocking, and settle down to what I tell myself is a well-earned rest. The next year is not very far away. And what then?

✍ Bibliography ❧

Blawer, Dian, *John Peck of Parson Drove: An Exceptional Fenman* (Wisbech & Fenland Museum, 1997)

Clayton, Peter, *Octavia Hill, 1838–1912* (Wisbech Society and Preservation Trust, 1993)

Cobbett, William, *Rural Rides* (vol.2) (Dent, 1912)

Darley, Gillian, *Octavia Hill: A Life* (Constable, 1990)

Kincaid, Sir John, *Random Shots from a Rifleman* (Murray, 1835)

Lehmann, Joseph, *Remember You Are An Englishman* (Cape, 1977)

Le Huray, Peter, *Music and the Reformation of England* (Jenkins, 1967)

McReynolds, Madeline, *The Peckovers of Wisbech* (Wisbech Society and Preservation Trust, 1994)

Pemberton, Max, *The Life of Sir Henry Royce* (Selwyn & Blount, 1954)

Purser, Audrey, *Thorpe Hall* (Sue Ryder Home, 1994)

Ryder, Lady Sue, *A Child of Love* (Collins Harvill, 1986)

Smith, Sir Harry, *Memoirs* (2 vols) (Murray, 1901)

Storey, Edward, *A Right to Song: A Life of John Clare* (Methuen, 1982)

Storey, Edward, *In Fen Country Heaven*, (Hale, 1996)

Traherne, Thomas, *Centuries of Meditations* (Oxford University Press, 1966)

University of Cambridge Board of Continuing Education, *Madingley Hall* a guide to the interior and exterior of the house, (1986)

Waszak, Peter, *The Nene Valley Railway* (Nene Valley Railway, 1990)

White, Gilbert, *The Natural History of Selborne*, (Dent, 1906)

Wilson, Ellen Gibson, *Jonathan Clarkson and the African Adventure* (Macmillan, 1980)

———, *Thomas Clarkson: A Biography* (Macmillan, 1989)

Wood, Jonathan, *The Rolls-Royce* (Octopus, 1982)

Wordsworth, Dorothy, *The Journals* (Oxford University Press, 1971)

ᙓ Index ᙡ